HOW TO MASTER LANGUAGES

In this Series

How to Apply for a Job
How to Apply to an Industrial Tribunal
How to Be a Freelance Secretary
How to Be a Local Councillor
How to Be an Effective School Governor
How to Buy & Run a Shop
How to Buy & Run a Small Hotel
How to Choose a Private School
How to Claim State Benefits
How to Conduct Staff Appraisals
How to Do Your Own Advertising
How to Employ & Manage Staff
How to Enjoy Retirement
How to Get a Job Abroad
How to Get a Job in America
How to Get a Job in Australia
How to Get a Job in Europe
How to Get a Job in France
How to Get That Job
How to Help Your Child at School
How to Invest in Stocks & Shares
How to Keep Business Accounts
How to Know Your Rights at Work
How to Know Your Rights: Patients
How to Know Your Rights: Students
How to Know Your Rights: Teachers
How to Live & Work in America
How to Live & Work in Australia
How to Live & Work in Belgium
How to Live & Work in Canada
How to Live & Work in France
How to Live & Work in Germany
How to Live & Work in Hong Kong
How to Live & Work in Italy
How to Live & Work in Japan
How to Live & Work in New Zealand
How to Live & Work in Portugal
How to Live & Work in Saudi Arabia
How to Live & Work in Spain
How to Lose Weight & Keep Fit

How to Make It in Films & TV
How to Manage a Sales Team
How to Manage Budgets & Cash Flows
How to Manage Computers at Work
How to Manage People at Work
How to Master Book-Keeping
How to Master Business English
How to Master GCSE Accounts
How to Master Languages
How to Master Public Speaking
How to Pass Exams Without Anxiety
How to Pass That Interview
How to Plan a Wedding
How to Prepare Your Child for School
How to Publish a Book
How to Publish a Newsletter
How to Raise Business Finance
How to Raise Funds & Sponsorship
How to Rent & Buy Property in France
How to Rent & Buy Property in Italy
How to Retire Abroad
How to Run a Local Campaign
How to Spend a Year Abroad
How to Start a Business from Home
How to Start a New Career
How to Study Abroad
How to Study & Live in Britain
How to Survive at College
How to Survive Divorce
How to Take Care of Your Heart
How to Teach Abroad
How to Understand Finance at Work
How to Use a Library
How to Work from Home
How to Work in an Office
How to Write a Press Release
How to Write a Report
How to Write an Essay
How to Write for Publication
How to Write for Television

Other titles in preparation

Master Languages

For business, study, travel and living abroad

Roger Jones

How To Books

British Library Cataloguing in Publication Data
A catalogue record for this book is available from the British Library.

© Copyright 1993 by Roger Jones
First published in 1991 as *Languages and How to Master Them*. Second edition (fully revised and re-set) published in 1993 by How To Books Ltd., Plymbridge House, Estover Road, Plymouth PL6 7PZ, United Kingdom. Tel: (0752) 735251/695745. Fax: (0752) 695699.Telex: 45635.

All rights reserved. No part of this work may be reproduced or stored in an information retrieval system (other than for purposes of review) without the express permission of the Publisher in writing.

Note: The material contained in this book is set out in good faith for general guidance and no liability can be accepted for loss or expense incurred as a result of relying in particular circumstances on statements made in the book. The law and regulations are complex and liable to change, and readers should check the current position with the relevant authorities before making personal arrangements.

Roger Alan Jones hereby asserts his moral right to be identified as the author of this work.

Typeset by Concept Typesetting Ltd., Salisbury, Wiltshire.
Printed and bound by The Cromwell Press, Broughton Gifford, Melksham, Wiltshire.

Preface

The purpose of this book is to encourage people to take up a foreign language and offer guidance on how to set about the task. It is targeted at would-be language learners and employers in the English-speaking world, rather than teachers or language experts who are already adequately catered for. Issues are tackled in a simple and clear-cut manner without recourse to jargon.

In addition to offering advice, the book has an extensive reference section which will also be of interest to language professionals, librarians and booksellers. In it I have listed course books which are readily available in the English-speaking world and should enable a would-be learner to get off to a good start. Inevitably there are omissions, partly for reasons of space, partly because the books may be difficult to obtain outside their country of origin, or simply because of lack of awareness on my part.

I have also included the addresses of organisations in the United Kingdom that are involved in language training. However, the list is by no means comprehensive; nor does inclusion on it signify endorsement by myself. Indeed, whether you are an individual seeking to take up a language or a company executive wishing to provide language training for your staff it is advisable to shop around. A first step is to discover what local educational and training institutions can offer before you look further afield.

Incidentally, I am always happy to receive information on good-quality language courses and training organisations which might be included in the reference section of future editions of this book.

A number of people and organisations have helped me in the preparation of this book, supplying me with information, allowing me to use their facilities or offering ideas and criticism, and I am extremely grateful to them. They include many of the publishers listed in Appendix B, Cheltenham Public Library,

CILT, LCL, Linguarama, London Chamber of Commerce and Industry, London University Institute of Education Library, OMTRAC, SOAS and Mrs Valerie Hodges.

Roger Jones

Contents

Preface		5
1	Why learn a foreign language?	9
2	Which language should I choose?	17
3	Language training and where to find it	26
4	Getting down to language learning	36
5	Issues and problems for the language learner	49
6	Children and language learning	73
7	Language training in organisations	82
Appendix A	Languages of the world. Details of course books and sources of information	94
Appendix B	Language course publishers and distributors	122
Appendix C	Useful addresses: course providers and miscellaneous	134
Appendix D	National languages: a country-by-country guide	145
Appendix E	Select bibliography	150
Appendix F	Language families	152
Index		155

1
Why Learn a Foreign Language?

'If you cannot speak a foreign language, you have no future in my country.' A stark prospect indeed!

The speaker was a Turk, and he was explaining why there is such enthusiasm for learning foreign languages in his country, with parents queuing up to enrol their children in bilingual Turkish–English schools. This enthusiasm has a pragmatic basis, since any Turk who wants to get on — to go abroad, to study, to get a good job — needs at least one foreign language in order to fulfil his ambitions.

The same is true for the natives of other countries I could mention — Norway, Hungary, Iceland, Yugoslavia, Greece, to name but a few. Any Athenian knows that — glorious though his language is — it is of limited use once he ventures beyond the national borders. If he goes on to higher education he will find that many of his textbooks are written in foreign languages. If he becomes an international businessman he will find his business negotiations are hardly ever conducted in Greek.

If you were born in the British Isles, much of North America and Australasia, you can consider yourself fortunate in at least one respect: you speak a major world language — English. Apart from being your national language, it is the official language of several other countries, such as India, Nigeria and Singapore.

English is widely used in international business, higher education and research, and plays a vital role in international communications including aviation. When you land at any international airport and check in at any large hotel, you will see signs written in English and find people who can speak English. If you attend an international conference, many of the delegates will converse with each other in English, and many of the speeches will use this medium.

What, then, is the point of learning another language, when English appears to be so widely used? The simple answer is that while the use of English is widespread, it is by no means the universal language. In South America a knowledge of Spanish or Portuguese will be more useful than a knowledge of English. And, while English may be the lingua franca in some parts of Africa, French or Portuguese will be of greater importance in others.

Some English-speakers assume that while knowledge of a foreign tongue is a desirable accomplishment, it is no more than that. This is a dangerous assumption in a world that is rapidly becoming more interdependent and where national boundaries are melting away. Britain's trade (as well as that of the Irish Republic) is no longer mainly with the English-speaking world, but with other countries of the European Community. North America and Australasia have developed strong links with their neighbours around the Pacific Rim. There seems to be much more contact with people from other non-English-speaking countries than there used to be.

As far as the British and Irish are concerned, our destinies will be linked to that of the European continent, where other languages are very well entrenched. It may come as a surprise to realise that German is the most widely spoken first language of western Europe as well as being an important lingua franca in south-eastern Europe; French, Italian and Spanish run English fairly close. As a consequence, there is little likelihood that English will be able to attain the same position of dominance in Europe as it did in the countries colonised by the British (including the United States).

'If [Europe] decides to make the most of its identity, it cannot be anything other than multilingual,' remarks Jean-Pierre van Deth (*Language International*, Vol. I:3, p. 9). In the light of this assertion, we need to respond to the concept of multilingualism with enthusiasm rather than with reluctance. Indeed we ignore other languages at our peril. Bacon's belief that 'knowledge itself is power' applies just as readily to the knowledge of foreign languages.

When foreign businessmen come to sell us their products and services, they speak to us in English. This is not because English is the language of Shakespeare and the lingua franca of commerce, but simply because they are likely to be more successful in landing contracts if they speak the language of their customers. For them speaking a foreign language makes sound commercial sense, and native English-speakers would do well to emulate them.

So far we have been talking about languages in general terms. Let us now look in greater detail at the benefits that learning a foreign language can bring.

THE BENEFITS

To foster business, political and cultural links
As mentioned above, the language of business is essentially the language of your customer, and he (or she) is more likely to take you seriously and buy your goods if you are able to speak to him in his own language. This is particularly true where your customer speaks no English at all — and there are plenty of them, particularly in the higher ranks of foreign companies.

To work through an interpreter is really only second best in such circumstances: it lessens the impact of your message and in addition you cannot always rely on the interpretation conveying your precise meaning. Even if you cannot converse in the language in question, you ought to have at least some passive understanding of it so as to be able to follow the drift of discussions you are involved in.

It is not just salesmen who need to have a knowledge of foreign languages. Some contracts involve the provision of technical support staff who need to be able to communicate with customers and their employees. Sometimes businessmen need to negotiate with governments and international organisations (such as the European Commission) to gain more favourable terms for their goods or services.

Professional organisations and public-sector bodies are increasingly in need of staff who are able to communicate well with their counterparts in other countries. The greater the effort put into improving communication skills the stronger the links that are likely to develop.

Language skills can also contribute to the success of bilateral and international exchanges. Many towns and districts in the British Isles are twinned with places on the European continent and arrange reciprocal visits by businessmen, students, young people and senior citizens.

To read foreign texts
English is generally looked upon as the international academic language. But does this necessarily remove the need for scholars and researchers to be able to handle other languages?

Not at all. More than half the world's scientific publications are written in languages other than English, according to a survey made in 1980, and it is possible that you will miss out on some vital piece of research in your field if you are monolingual.

A great deal of important research is conducted in Japan and the

German-speaking world, but by no means all the papers are published in English. I sometimes wonder whether the Japanese are now overtaking the West in technical matters simply because their scientists and engineers can read papers in English whereas the number of Western professionals that can cope with Japanese is decidedly small.

To understand a country and its people
The tradition of learning other languages so as to have access to the literature of other countries has been in place for centuries, and many of the modern language courses in higher education continue to boast a considerable literary component.

The literature of a country is often a key to understanding national attitudes, but usually only a small proportion of the literary output is available in English translation and that may not be a particularly representative sample. If you want to get to grips with Romanian literature, you really need to know Romanian.

Nowadays, with increasing contact between countries, the desire (and need) to know about other cultures has never been greater. In previous centuries we tended to concentrate our attention on the countries of Europe, while the rest of the world tended to remain the preserve of scholars. Now we are looking further afield — to find out about the Arab world, Africa, China and Japan.

Documents such as government records, newspapers and religious treatises are even less likely to appear in English translation, and this means that historians, sociologists, anthropologists, journalists and others who do not speak the language of the country find themselves at a disadvantage: their understanding is incomplete.

However, the study of other nations should not be merely the concern of scholars and opinion formers. Anyone who comes into regular contact with foreign nationals needs to make it his business to scan their newspapers, watch their films, read their books and listen to their opinions in order to understand their view of the world.

To cope with periods of residence abroad
If you are posted to a foreign country for any length of time it is sensible to acquire some knowledge of the national or local language.

You will then be able to cope more easily with daily tasks, such as shopping, answering the door or the telephone, asking for directions, and handling emergencies. More importantly you will feel more at ease in your new surroundings: you will have some inkling as to what people are talking about and be able to communicate with them, albeit imperfectly.

Until you overcome the linguistic hurdle there is a danger that you will feel an outsider. Though your work may not require a knowledge of the national language, you may find at the social level your inability to converse is a handicap. When your colleagues relax, they quite naturally fall back into conversing with one another in their mother tongue, and you will feel something of an outsider if you cannot participate properly.

Ignorance of the local language can pose even bigger problems for accompanying dependants. They can feel isolated when left at home all day in unfamiliar surroundings with no English-speaking neighbours in sight to strike up an acquaintance with. Sadly, a substantial number of foreign contracts are terminated prematurely not because the employee himself fails to cope, but because his dependants fail to come to terms with their new environment.

For travel and recreation

A great many people attend evening language classes or follow language courses on radio because they are planning to visit a particular country on holiday.

Certainly some knowledge of the language can add greatly to the enjoyment of the holiday. It will help you buy what you want in restaurants, hotels, garages and shops and get you to your destination on the local transport services. You will be able to get the gist of films, plays and other spectacles, and make the most of museums and cultural sites where the labelling is only in the national tongue.

For many people part of the charm of a holiday is the people they meet. With their language at your command you should be able to develop a much closer relationship with the local people and gain an insight into their ideas and attitudes.

You will doubtless be able to survive with English in large cities and resorts, but in the more remote areas — which are often more picturesque and interesting — there is less likelihood of your finding an English-speaker who can smooth your path.

As an intellectual challenge

Some people like to learn a language for its own sake — as a means of exercising the grey cells — rather than for any practical purpose. And why not?

In the past, study of classical languages was regarded as an indispensable part of a person's education, as Latin and Greek were supposed to foster logical thinking. To attain proficiency in either certainly indicates a high degree of commitment and concentration, and the same must surely apply to the acquisition of other tongues.

It is also widely held that mastery of other languages can often lead to a richer vocabulary and greater precision in one's own. Shakespeare, with his 'little Latin and less Greek', is surely a model for us all.

To maintain contact with one's 'roots'

There are millions of second- and third-generation immigrants in English-speaking countries whose parents or grandparents were born in countries where another language was spoken. While they are proud to be citizens of the United Kingdom, Canada, Australia, New Zealand or the United States, they do not want to lose contact completely with their family origins.

Canada, in particular, is making an effort to provide language tuition in ethnic minority languages, such as Ukrainian and Polish, and in Britain there are countless groups either providing or pressing for facilities for learning Asian and African languages.

To assist you in your career

Proficiency in at least one foreign language is generally regarded as a plus by employers, even if the position you have applied for does not seem to require foreign language skills. Most firms and organisations — from manufacturers to tour operators — have foreign connections of some kind or another: they receive communications in foreign languages and need to deal with foreign clients, not all of whom speak English.

As you move up the career ladder, there may be chances for promotion or secondment abroad. Many firms — banks, computer service operations, insurance companies, manufacturers and so on — are international operations these days with branches or representations in several other countries. It is clearly in their interests to send out someone who can speak to customers in their own language.

This could well be a different language from the one you have learned, but that is not a problem. If you have managed to learn one language, your employers will reason that you have the aptitude to learn another, and may well be prepared to finance an intensive language training course before you go.

Forward-looking firms are increasingly aware of the need to

develop managers with a cosmopolitan outlook. As a consequence several now send management trainees for language training. A major tobacco firm, for instance, sends selected trainees on Arabic courses before posting them to the Arab world; others are giving staff appointed to Tokyo a grounding in Japanese.

In some types of work you need to use a foreign language to deal with people in your own country who are not conversant with English, as would be the case with a hotel receptionist or tour guide, or with a social worker or teacher involved with ethnic minorities.

For a career using languages

In the previous section we considered foreign language ability as a secondary skill at work. Languages are important, but they take second place to marketing, administration, accountancy and other areas of expertise.

However, in certain careers languages play a central role. Here are the main ones:

- *Interpreting.* This can be a very varied career which could range from accompanying a group of businessmen abroad to interpreting for the police. However, the number of vacancies for interpreters with large companies and international organisations is fairly limited, there being only about 1,500 full-time conference interpreters in the world.

- *Translating.* There is a particular need for technical translators who can render manuals, reports, letters and other documents into good, clear prose. Vacancies occur in government, international organisations (especially the European Community which runs regular competitions for translators) and large companies. Many translators are freelance and may have a link-up with a translation agency.

    Normally translators are required to translate from the foreign language into their mother tongue, and a high degree of accuracy is called for. While computers are being used increasingly in translation, they cannot yet achieve 100 per cent accuracy, and so humans are still needed to edit and polish up machine translation.

- *Abstractors and monitors.* Libraries and information services employ a limited number of linguists to abstract and classify foreign texts. Linguists are also required by the Government Communications Headquarters (GCHQ) and the BBC Monitoring Service to monitor and report on foreign language transmissions and broadcasts.

- *Teaching languages.* Teaching is the largest employer of language graduates, and currently there is a shortage of modern language teachers at all levels both in the public and private sectors.

THE NEXT STEP

So what is *your* motive in learning a foreign language? Does it correspond to one of the reasons given above or is it quite different? Is your ultimate aim business or pleasure?

It is important to clarify your aims right from the start. Only when you have done so, can you decide on your level of commitment in terms of time, effort and expenditure. Your motives for learning may also determine the way you learn.

HOW TO TEACH ABROAD
Roger Jones

'An excellent book... An exhaustive and practical coverage of the possibilities and practicalities of teaching overseas.' *The Escape Committee Newsletter.* 'This comprehensive and well-researched guidebook would be an invaluable asset for anyone contemplating teaching abroad, whether in the EC, the Commonwealth countries, or further afield... Offers a great deal of very practical advice'... *Education.* 'A comprehensive guide — well set out and user friendly... This is a useful, relatively cheap addition to any careers library, that I can recommend.' *Phoenix/Association of Graduate Careers Advisory Services.* Roger Jones has himself worked abroad in Austria, Cambodia, Thailand, Turkey and the Middle East.

£6.99, 176pp illus. 0 7463 0551 6.

Please add postage & packing (UK £1.00 per copy. Europe £2.00 per copy. World £3.00 per copy airmail).
How To Books Ltd, Plymbridge House, Estover Road, Plymouth PL6 7PZ, United Kingdom. Tel: (0752) 695745. Fax: (0752) 695699. Telex: 45635.

2
Which Language Should I Choose?

There are countless languages in the world. In Appendix A I list some of them, but they represent only a small selection of the languages spoken in the world. In Africa alone there are estimated to be 1,000 different tongues, some of which may be spoken by only a few hundred people. Others are facing extinction, as has been the fate of Cornish and Manx.

While comparisons may be odious it has to be admitted that some languages are more important than others. If we judge the importance of a language by the number of people for whom it is their mother tongue, the top ten languages are as follows: Mandarin Chinese, the mother tongue of 750 million people; English (300 million); Hindi-Urdu (220 million); Spanish (200 million); Arabic (180 million); Russian (170 million); Portuguese (160 million); Bengali (150 million); Japanese (120 million); German (120 million). The numbers are very approximate.

So does this mean that we need to concentrate our efforts on learning Chinese, Bengali and Hindi and forget about French? Not a bit of it. French is, after all, an important lingua franca and the official language of a good many states in Africa and elsewhere. Bengali and Hindi are important languages on the Indian subcontinent and among Asian communities overseas, but neither is an international lingua franca. Indeed, English is more widely used in the region than these two Indo-Aryan languages.

THE TEN MOST USEFUL FOREIGN LANGUAGES FOR AN ENGLISH-SPEAKER

Languages are meant to be used, and your first consideration is whether there is a language you are definitely going to need in the future. I would not normally urge people to learn Finnish, although it happens to be a very interesting language. But if you hear that you are to be posted to Finland for a couple of years, getting to grips with the national language should be one of your priorities.

Similarly, missionaries in Thailand learn the languages of the hill tribespeople because they will be working with them.

Arabic

Arabic is the national language of some 20 countries in the Arab world, which stretches from Morocco in the west to Oman in the east. It is also the language of Islam, and therefore of great interest to Muslims throughout the world, whether they live in Bangladesh, Brunei or Bradford.

But of what relevance is Arabic to English-speakers? For one thing, most English-speaking countries have strong trading links with the Arab world; the countries of the Arabian peninsula, in particular, are important export markets. Furthermore, because of its strategic position we in the West need to understand the culture of the area and the attitudes of the people, and an understanding of the language is surely the key to this.

A final consideration is that the Arab world is an important source of employment. The richer Arab states need foreign expertise to build up their infrastructure, and there are tens of thousands of expatriates (many of them from English-speaking countries) working in Saudi Arabia alone — on construction projects, in the oil and gas industry, in trading companies, etc. I have no doubt whatsoever that an expatriate who speaks the language will be more successful in his work and derive more satisfaction from his job if he can converse with the locals in their own language.

Yet it has to be admitted that Arabic is not an easy language to learn. Its grammar is different from that of most Western European languages, and so is its vocabulary, pronunciation and writing system. Moreover, there are many varieties of Arabic and it is sometimes difficult to know which to concentrate on. However, if you are likely to be spending some time in the Arab world or wish to know more about the area and Islam, it is a language you cannot ignore.

Chinese

In terms of sheer numbers Chinese is by far the most important language in the world. Mandarin (Putonghua) is the national language of the Chinese People's Republic and Taiwan (Nationalist China), and one of the official languages in Singapore. Cantonese is the language of Hong Kong, of Macao and probably of the proprietor of your local Chinese restaurant! Chinese in one of its guises is used by the large and dynamic Chinese communities

Which Language Should I Choose?

residing in the countries of South-East Asia and elsewhere in the world.

Because of the dominant commercial position of the Chinese in eastern Asia it makes sense for businessmen to be able to converse in the language. China is a regional power, if not a world power, and it is important for us to know how the people are thinking through Chinese newspapers and other publications. For the scholar, Chinese is an important literary language of a civilisation that goes back thousands of years.

But is is also to the Western mind one of the most inaccessible languages because of its script with its seemingly infinite number of characters. Even if you abandon any idea of learning the script, the pronunciation of Chinese can also cause problems. It may take years to become really proficient in both the spoken and the written language, and you may well be able to polish off two or three European languages in the time that takes.

Clearly if you are going to spend time in eastern Asia a knowledge of Chinese will prove an asset. However, the canny Chinese are also adept at learning English, and non-Chinese-speakers can certainly get around with just a few basic words.

Japanese

Japanese deserves consideration in this section because of Japan's position as a leading industrial power. There are many opportunities for exporting to Japan, provided that you are prepared to make the effort; and this involves getting to grips with the language as well as the customs of the country.

Another consideration is that Japanese companies are setting up plants and branches all over the world, with the result that an increasing number of English-speaking people are finding themselves employees of Japanese firms. One pointer to the future is a move by at least one English county council to introduce Japanese teaching into its schools, because a major Japanese company has come to the area. It surely makes sense to be able to speak the language of your boss.

Even if Toyota doesn't move to your locality, an increasing number of companies in Europe and North America are embarking on joint ventures with the Japanese, for which a knowledge of the language would be a definite asset. Also, with an increasing number of Japanese tourists opting for foreign holidays, hotels and tourist agencies need staff who can speak their clients' tongue.

A final consideration is the Japanese tradition of academic excellence. An increasing number of scientific and technical reports are written in Japanese, and companies and research establishments ignore them at their peril. For the scholar Japan has a very rich literary tradition.

Yet Japanese is somewhat daunting with its three writing systems, two alphabetic, the other based on Chinese characters. Fortunately the pronunciation is not too much of a problem, and the grammatical structure, while unlike that of European languages, has the merit of being fairly regular. If you think you are likely to have dealings with the Japanese, the language is well worth considering.

French

Normally when foreign languages are talked about, French is the first that comes to mind. A large number of English speakers have learned French at school, and it continues to be by far the most popular foreign language in the British Isles, perhaps because France is the foreign country which is closest to our shores.

It remains an important international lingua franca, though its status as the language of diplomacy has diminished during the last fifty years. It is the official language of a least twenty countries around the world and understood in a good many others. If one wants to do commerce with France and other French-speaking countries a knowledge of the language will prove a tremendous asset. It is also an important language for academic and technological works.

A good many people learn French for pleasure, and why not? French films, French literature, French songs and French cuisine are much admired throughout the world, and France itself is a popular holiday destination, particularly among the British. The language is also a useful tool if you are planning holidays in Spain, Portugal, Italy or North Africa.

French is not the easiest of languages to speak or spell, but the vocabulary should not present too many problems, since half of the words in English have come from Norman French or other Romance tongues. There are countless opportunities for learning the language.

German

German is the second most commonly taught language in Britain after French and its usefulness is not in doubt. Germany is the leading economic power in Europe and a major trading partner, so if you are keen to do business with Germany it makes sense to learn the language. The same holds true for the other German-speaking countries, Austria and Switzerland. Another consideration is that you may well be working for the subsidiary of a German or Swiss firm.

German is a European language rather than an international one, but its use is not confined to the countries mentioned above. If you visit Eastern Europe on business or for pleasure you will find German a useful lingua franca, particularly in Yugoslavia, Hungary, Bulgaria, Greece and Turkey. One reason is that a good many people from these countries have worked as *Gastarbeiter* or studied in Germany in the past.

Many people study German for cultural reasons. German is a major literary language which figures very prominently in music as well as being an important medium for disseminating scientific information thanks to the high reputation of universities and research institutes in the German-speaking world. And, while tourists may not be drawn to the industrial cities of Germany, the Rhine and southern Germany are popular with visitors, while both Austria and Switzerland are major tourist destinations.

German is closely related to English, and though its genders, word order and inflections may cause difficulties it is well within the grasp of an average learner. Besides, there are plenty of opportunities to learn German and visit German-speaking countries.

Italian

Italian may not rank as an international language, but it is popular among language learners. Its geographical spread is limited and there is little commercial advantage to the language unless you happen to be involved in trade with Italy or the various Italian communities around the world, notably in the United States.

Italian's great attraction is essentially cultural. As the cradle of the Renaissance, Italy attracts millions of visitors each year, and while a good many people in the tourist industry speak English you will enjoy the atmosphere of the place far more if you can converse with the locals in their own tongue. Italian literature is also much appreciated, and so is Italian opera, which always sounds so much better when sung in the original language. Italian is *par excellence* the language of art and music.

Though Italian may not be a major language in any political sense it is worth while including it in one's portfolio of languages. Moreover, it is fairly easy to learn, particularly if you already know French.

Latin

'Latin is a language as dead as dead can be.
It killed the Ancient Romans and now it's killing me.'

Latin may seem out of place in a manual of this kind — a relic of the past rather than a medium for commercial transactions. Even so, the language is still widely studied in Britain, although its popularity has certainly waned during the past twenty-five years.

At one time it was argued that learning Latin was a good way of training the mind. This may be so, but even today Latin has a practical application. No historian of Western Europe from Roman times till the eighteenth century can afford to ignore it, since a good deal of documentation prior to the modern period is written in Latin. In the Middle Ages it was the lingua franca of scholarship throughout Christendom, and it still plays an important unifying role in the Roman Catholic Church of today. Apart from these considerations Latin has a very rich literature which not only is well worth studying but also has exerted considerable influence on European language and culture up to the present time.

Portuguese

Portugal is one of the smaller countries of Europe, so why is its language considered so important? The answer, of course, is: Brazil. Brazil, with its 120 million or so Portuguese-speakers, is the giant of the South American continent, and should offer excellent trading opportunities when it eventually sorts out its economy. The language is also spoken in former Portuguese possessions in Africa, notably in Mozambique and Angola, both countries with considerable economic potential. Other places where Portuguese is still spoken are Macao and Goa.

You might use your knowledge of Portuguese to read the considerable body of literature in the language or on a holiday in Portugal. The language is fairly close to Spanish and both languages are mutually intelligible.

Russian

This is a major world language by reason of the number of people who speak it as a first or second language and because of the political importance of Russia. It is a useful lingua franca throughout Eastern Europe, where the majority of languages are Slavonic and thus closely related to Russian, and it is not unusual to find Russian-speakers in Third World countries who have attended universities in the former USSR.

Which Language Should I Choose?

With the end of the Cold War there is every prospect of greater interchange between the West and Russia in terms of both trade and cultural relations, and this will increase the usefulness of Russian. Russian is also worth learning for its extensive literature, both literary and scientific.

Yet of all the European languages Russian seems the most forbidding. The first obstacle is the Cyrillic script; the second is the pronunciation (difficult consonant clusters, knowing where to put the stress); the third the many inflections (word endings). It is not a language to be picked up in a hurry, but once learned it is relatively easy to proceed to other Slavonic languages.

Spanish

In the Western Hemisphere Spanish is the second most important language after English, being the language of Central and South America, of much of the Caribbean, and of sizeable Spanish communities in the United States itself. As a global lingua franca it stands with French in second place after English. It is of considerable interest whether you are a businessman, tourist or lover of literature.

Fortunately, it is also relatively easy to learn, particularly if you know French or Latin. The spelling is logical; the vocabulary reasonably familiar; and there is ample opportunity to practise it.

OTHER USEFUL FOREIGN LANGUAGES

If you speak all ten of the languages mentioned in addition to your own, you should be able to communicate in any part of the world. There are, however, other major languages which are worth considering.

Relations with Eastern Europe are going to strengthen with the passing of the Cold War, and certainly tourism to these countries is going to increase. Visitors to the Adriatic will find a knowledge of **Serbo-Croat** well worth while, and languages such as **Polish, Czech, Slovak** and **Hungarian** will doubtless increase in importance in the business world.

Of the southern European languages not mentioned so far, **Greek** is worth considering, not least because Greece is a favourite tourist venue these days. For a scholar or theologian a knowledge of Classical or New Testament Greek is a must. **Turkish** is also worth considering for reasons not only of tourism but also of business. It is also a fascinating language in its own right and related to other languages of Asia Minor.

Further to the East **Persian** is worth thinking about. Admittedly in the eighties both Iran and Afghanistan have been somewhat isolated, but there are now signs of a thaw in relations between both countries and the West.

As the national language of India and Pakistan, **Hindi-Urdu** is clearly of major importance in the subcontinent, though **Bengali** predominates in the east and is the national language of Bangladesh. The Indian languages are also of importance to people working with Asian ethnic minorities.

In South-East Asia there are a number of languages worth considering. **Indonesian-Malay** is widely spoken in Malaysia and Indonesia, both important economies, and has the merit of being easy to learn. **Thai**, by contrast, is more demanding on the learner, but is understood in Laos and northern Burma as well as Thailand itself.

Now that Vietnam has started to concentrate on building up its economy, **Vietnamese** could well be of importance: it is certainly important for people working with refugees from the area. Finally, if one considers that Korea to the north is on its way to becoming a second Japan in economic terms, the study of **Korean** could prove rewarding.

On the continent of Africa there are so many languages that it is difficult to know which ones to choose. Of the non-European languages used, **Hausa** is the major lingua franca in West Africa and **Swahili** in East Africa, and the latter has a reputation of being an easy language. Missionary and volunteer groups are particularly active in this region, and if you are keen to work in development a knowledge of the local language (as opposed to the official language of the country) will prove very useful.

By singling out certain languages there is a danger that people will consider those not mentioned as inferior or of no use. Perish the thought! All languages are worth learning if you know there is a chance of being able to use them. Languages are, after all, meant to be used rather than just studied.

Hence, in the British Isles, if you are planning to live in the west of Ireland or the north-west of Scotland, it would be highly desirable to have a crack at learning the local version of **Gaelic**. Not everybody does so, however, since it is not strictly necessary: everybody in these regions speaks perfect English as a first or second language.

On the other hand if you are a social worker working with ethnic minorities in a major city you might find it very useful to learn the language of a particular community because many of its older members do not speak English.

Which Language Should I Choose?

Whether you are going to work with a particular community at home or in a foreign country for a time, make sure you choose the right language. Not every Pakistani speaks Urdu, nor every Chinese Mandarin. Switzerland has four different languages and there is little point in learning German if you are heading for Geneva or Lugano.

HOW TO GET A JOB ABROAD
Roger Jones

This top-selling title is essential for everyone planning to spend a period abroad. It contains a big reference section of medium and long-term job opportunities and possibilities, arranged by region and country of the world, and by profession/occupation. There are more than 130 pages of specific contacts and leads, giving literally hundreds of addresses and much hard-to-find information. There is a classified guide to overseas recruitment agencies, and even a multilingual guide to writing application letters. 'A fine book for anyone considering even a temporary overseas job.' *The Evening Star.* 'A highly informative and well researched book... containing lots of hard information and a first class reference section... A superb buy.' *The Escape Committe Newsletter.* 'A valuable addition to any careers library.' *Phoenix (Association of Graduate Careers Advisory Services).* Roger Jones has himself worked abroad for many years and is a specialist writer on expatriate and employment matters.

£9.99, 288pp illus. 1 85703 003 6.

Please add postage & packing (UK £1.00 per copy. Europe £2.00 per copy. World £3.00 per copy airmail).
How To Books Ltd, Plymbridge House, Estover Road, Plymouth PL6 7PZ, United Kingdom. Tel: (0752) 695745. Fax: (0752) 695699. Telex: 45635.

3
Language Training and Where to Find It

Some time back a German friend of mine decided to brush up his English and enrolled for a course in his home town. But the experience proved frustrating rather than enlightening, since most of his fellow students were elderly folk who seemed to regard their lessons as a social occasion rather than as an opportunity to better themselves. He was an intelligent young man who wanted to get on with his studies, but the teacher had to fall in with the wishes of the majority and so progress was slow.

His experience serves to highlight a factor that every potential language student has to bear in mind. There are courses and courses, some of which will suit you, and others which will not. If your fellow students share your motivation and your teacher is able to meet your aspirations, there should be little to worry about. But if the class is excessively heterogeneous — containing people with differing aims, abilities and inclinations — the teacher has to balance the interests of one group against those of the others and perhaps reach a compromise that satisfies no-one.

A course which prepares its students for an examination is likely to be more rigorous than one that does not. On the other hand, such a course may have its limitations as far as you yourself are concerned. If your principal aim is oral competence and the course leads to a written examination, you may find that too much attention is paid to reading or writing skills.

In order to start off on the right foot you need to do some homework before you commit yourself to a course of language learning. Chapter 1 should have helped you to decide what your objectives are in learning a language. Now we have to understand what you are letting yourself in for and the constraints you have to take into account.

COURSE LENGTH, FREQUENCY AND TYPE

How long does it take to become proficient in a language? This is a good question. Pupils in state schools in the United Kingdom

Language Training and Where to Find It

normally study French for five years before taking their GCSE exams and even then many are lost for words when they encounter a native of France. By contrast, students at London University may achieve a reasonable competence in Italian in just one month.

Why this difference? While superior brain power and motivation may be two of the students' assets, there are several others: they are taught in small groups, the course is intensive, they can concentrate wholly on the task in hand, Italian is relatively easy to learn, and they are already fluent in a related language. Given similar conditions, most other people would make good progress as well.

It is essential to stop thinking in terms of how long a course lasts and concentrate on how many hours of input it offers. The average adult education centre language course lasts perhaps 30 weeks, but at the rate of perhaps one lesson of one and a half hours per week this amounts to a mere 45 hours' tuition over the year. The university students receive more than double that amount of language input in four weeks.

A good many language teaching organisations think in terms of hours when estimating the effort needed to reach a certain level in the language. Manchester Business School reckons that to attain minimum oral competence it takes one month comprising 24 hours of class work plus 30 to 45 minutes a day home study, say 40 hours in total. One needs to bear in mind that it can take a good deal longer to reach an adequate standard in Arabic or Chinese than in a European language. In Appendix A I attempt to grade languages according to level of difficulty.

Clearly the more time you can devote to learning a language the quicker you will learn. Four hours a week is better than two; while one hour a day will be even better. People tend to forget more easily if there is a long interval between each lesson, so the more frequently you are exposed to the target language, the more effectively and quickly you will learn it.

Of course the more lessons you cram into a week the more it will cost in time and effort, and this cost has to be balanced against your other commitments. Many high-ranking businessmen from Europe are quite happy to spend a fortnight or a month doing an expensive intensive English course in Britain because it will quickly increase their fluency and hence prove to be a good investment. I believe we in the English-speaking world have to take a leaf out of their book.

In the next section attention is given to the types of course available from the various language course providers. When approaching them for information it is important to know what constraints you are operating under. Here are some questions to ask yourself.

- Can I commit myself to regular study?
  If the answer is yes, you could get in touch with any provider in categories 1 to 6. If no, you should consider category 7, 8 or 9.

- Do I need to learn a language quickly?
  If you do, some institutions in categories 1, 4, 5 and 6 offer intensive courses. Alternatively you could enrol for a course abroad (category 10).

- Are there financial constraints?
  If there are, it is worth bearing in mind that public sector organisations (especially categories 1, 2 and 5) tend to be less expensive than the other alternatives. Some local authorities are prepared to reduce or even waive fees for people in straitened circumstances.

- Do I need some form of certification?
  A language qualification can look very impressive on a CV, but not all courses are examination-oriented. Categories 1, 3, 4, 5, 6 and 8 are more likely than not to do so.

- Do I really want to learn a language as a form of recreation?
  If the answer is yes, consider categories 2, 5, 9 and 10.

- Is my firm prepared to finance my language learning?
  Far-sighted organisations are keener than they used to be with regard to language training. If yours is keen to support you, consider categories 4, 5, 6, 7 and 10. Some of the larger institutions in category 1 may also be worth approaching. See also Chapter 7.

COURSE PROVIDERS

1. Colleges of further education and technical colleges

Most colleges have departments of modern languages and arrange courses geared to certain examinations, e.g. Institute of Linguists or 'A' Level. They tend to confine themselves to the more common European languages, though some of the larger and more forward-looking ones might offer courses in Oriental languages such as

Arabic or Chinese. Normally course enrolment occurs early in September and the courses continue throughout the academic year provided the number of students does not fall below a certain level. Note that courses will vary in intensity and more flexible learning arrangements may be possible. Some institutions offer open access learning.

It is worth while contacting colleges in your area as a first step to find out what is on offer. Even if there is no course to suit your needs, you may be able to get information on some other training providers.

Course brochures for part-time courses are usually published in the summer and are obtainable from the colleges themselves. Training Access Points can provide information on work-related courses, including language courses. Public libraries and Job Centres have access to a training database at the Training Agency, St Mary's House, Moorfoot, Sheffield S1 4PQ. Tel: (0742) 527344.

2. Adult education centres and community colleges

Some adult education centres have their own premises while others are based within further education colleges or schools. They are geared to the needs of the adult learner; their courses are normally part-time and often take place in the evening. Londoners are particularly well placed when it comes to learning a foreign language: adult institutes around the capital organise courses in more than fifty languages, including Cornish, Romany and even Tigrinya!

Elsewhere the choice may be more limited, but adult education staff are often willing to respond to special requests. Normally enrolment takes place at the beginning of September and the courses continue throughout the academic year. A number of centres in larger cities offer courses in the languages of ethnic minorities, short courses, weekend courses and intensive courses.

Most brochures on courses are published in the late summer and are available from public libraries as well as adult education centres and adult education departments of local education authorities.

Floodlight, the official guide to part-time and evening courses in London, is published by the Association of London Authorities, 36 Old Queen Street, London SW1H 9JF. Tel: (071) 222 7799. For a full list of Adult Education Centres consult the *Educational Centres Association Directory* (Educational Centres Association, Chequer Centre, London EC1V 8PL. Tel: (071) 251 4158).

A few of the centres offering a particularly wide range of

language courses are listed in Appendix 6.

3. Residential adult colleges

There are two types of public sector college, one offering long-term courses often directed towards public examinations, and the other offering short courses (anything between two days and three weeks) in a wide range of subjects including languages. However, certain of the long-term colleges offer short courses as well: Coleg Harlech, for instance, offers a short course in Welsh during the summer. Other organisations, such as management colleges, also offer short residential courses.

The best sources of information on residential courses are: *Time to Learn — Residential Short Courses* (National Institute of Continuing Education, 19b De Montfort Street, Leicester LE1 7GE. Tel: (0533) 551451).

Courses for Leisure (Trotman & Co., 12–14 Hill Rise, Richmond, Surrey TW10 6UA. Tel: (081) 940 5668). See also Appendix C.

4. Universities, polytechnics and colleges of higher education

Most higher education institutions offer undergraduate courses in modern languages. The more traditional ones tend to have a literary bias while others (often in polytechnics) may be more business oriented. Undergraduate studies are dealt with in Linda Hantrais' book, *The Undergraduate's Guide to Studying Languages* (CILT).

In addition to providing three- or four-year degree programmes and postgraduate study, some universities and colleges organise shorter language courses that lead to certificates or diplomas; Thames Valley University (Ealing), for instance, offer a one-year intensive diploma course in Chinese for graduates.

However, most adults have to be content with part-time courses. In many universities these are organised by the Department of Extra-Mural Studies (sometimes called the Department of Continuing Education); in others there may be a special language centre which offers courses (standard or tailor-made) to the general public as at King's College, London.

Not all such courses are held on university premises. The University of Bristol, for instance, organises courses at centres spread through four counties. A typical course will start in early October and run for one, two or three terms. However, some departments provide short intensive courses, weekend courses and residential summer schools.

Institutions which offer expertise in certain less common

languages include the University College of Wales, Aberystwyth, in Welsh and the School of Oriental and African Studies (SOAS), London, in non-European languages. Some can provide a range of learning packages to the general public, or be able to suggest places where you can study your target language.

Brochures can be obtained by writing to the Department of Extra-Mural Studies (Department of Continuing Education or Language Centre) of the institution concerned, but local public libraries often have a stock of course brochures, too.

Guide to Language Courses in Polytechnics and Similar Institutions (Standing Conference of Heads of Modern Languages, University of Central Lancashire, Preston PR1 2TQ) is useful for reference.

Macmillan-PICKUP National Training Directory (Macmillan).

Summer Academy: Study Holidays at British Universities (School of Continuing Education, University of Kent, Canterbury CT2 7NX. Tel: (0227) 470402).

5. Cultural and educational organisations

Although public-sector language course provision is fairly extensive in Britain there are a good many other providers. Some of the best language courses are provided by foreign cultural institutes which usually have some official or semi-official status — not unlike the British Council, which operates English language centres abroad. Among the leading ones are the French Institute in London and Edinburgh, the (German) Goethe Institut — which has branches in London, Manchester, Glasgow and York — and the Spanish Institute.

Courses are also run by organisations which aim to promote interest in different countries and cultures, such as the Society for Anglo-Chinese Understanding, the Africa Centre and the Institute of Indian Culture. The Workers' Educational Association is also in the business of language courses and it would be worth contacting your nearest branch to find out what is on offer in your particular locality.

Finally, for retired people, the University of the Third Age may organise informal language groups in your area. The national address is: 1 Stockwell Green, London SW9 9JF. Tel: (071) 737 2541.

6. Private language schools

Well over a hundred years ago Maximilian Berlitz had the idea of setting up his first language school, and since then he has had thousands of imitators. Schools are either individually owned or form part of a chain; which may or may not adopt a particular method of teaching, such as the Berlitz Method, the Inlingua Method, etc. In many the emphasis in on acquiring listening and speaking skills.

Generally speaking, language schools tend to be more flexible than public-sector bodies and offer both intensive and non-intensive courses. Premises may seem smarter and more conducive to language learning than some of the enormous public sector institutions which seem to be all corridors and cavernous classrooms. A few are residential.

To find a private school look through your local Yellow Pages telephone directory to discover which institutions exist in your district. The publication *Where and How?* (Wie und Wo Verlag) lists a selection of language schools, as does Appendix C. You may also find that some colleagues or friends can recommend an establishment.

7. Private tutors

If there are no courses in your target language in your particular area, or you have difficulty in fitting in with whatever ones there are, private tuition should be considered. With a good private teacher you can proceed at your own pace and concentrate on the matters most appropriate to your needs. A business person, for instance, will be interested in developing a business vocabulary.

Some tutors will be prepared to come and teach you in your own home, or you may have to go to theirs. In order to share the cost there is no reason why two or more people should not join together to hire a tutor provided you are more or less at the same standard in the language in question.

However, you need to choose your tutor with care. It is wrong to assume that anyone who speaks the language can teach it. A native speaker may have little idea of the difficulties foreigners encounter when learning his language; even less on how to overcome them.

The person you choose needs to have some experience of teaching adults using up-to-date methods and be prepared to conduct much of the lesson in the target language. He (or she) should ideally be someone who inspires confidence and with whom you feel at ease.

To locate a tutor you can contact either a local educational establishment or public library to see if they can recommend anyone. Language teachers' associations can also help. See Appendix C.

8. Distance learning institutions

It is possible to learn a foreign language without leaving your home thanks to the BBC and other broadcasting organisations. Over the years the BBC in particular has developed a range of television and radio language courses for the commoner European languages as well as Arabic, Chinese and Hindi. To derive the maximum benefit from the broadcasts it is sensible to purchase a course book, and in some cases adult education centres organise courses based on these series.

Correspondence colleges also provide courses in languages, usually aimed at preparing people for examinations. Generally speaking, the emphasis is mainly, or perhaps entirely, on the written language. However, some organisations, such as the National Extension College, incorporate a spoken element in their courses. The Open College and Open University also offer language courses.

Telephone tutorials are yet another form of distance learning and they are becoming popular with people who are forever on the move. A number of private organisations, such as Linguaphone and Speak-Easy, are able to offer this facility, which can prove expensive.

Contact the BBC for details of its language course programming plans.

For details of correspondence colleges contact the Council for the Accreditation of Correspondence Colleges, 27 Marylebone Road, London NW1 5JS. Tel: (071) 935 5391.

9. Self-study

This is the most difficult option for a learner and demands a high level of motivation. In the past the only material a person could rely on was a textbook, which was sufficient if your principal aim was to learn how to read and write the language.

However, oral competence is prized more greatly and many of the more recent courses go some way to meeting this demand by offering tapes of the text either as an integral part of the course or as an extra. In addition, for the more popular languages it may be possible to obtain videos and computer programmes designed to stimulate interest and check your progress.

Clearly if you are aiming for oral competence in a language the more practice you have in speaking and writing it the better. Linguaphone is perhaps the best-known name in the field, but there is also excellent material available from the US Foreign

Service Institute, and a number of other publishers cater very adequately for the more popular languages.

Yet learning by yourself and speaking to yourself is a very artificial way of learning a language. You really need to find someone you can practise the language on and who can give you constructive feedback. See if there is a short course you can attend — a weekend course at an adult residential college, for instance — or pay a visit to the country where the language is spoken.

Consult the appropriate language section in Appendix A and investigate the range of materials mentioned in order to find a course that suits your purposes. In the case of the less commonly taught languages it would be sensible to contact a specialist or academic bookseller (some of which are listed in Appendix C).

COURSES ABROAD

This is an expensive option, since you have accommodation as well as tuition expenses, yet it could prove to be the most effective study option of all, since you have an opportunity to practise what you have learned outside the classroom. But to reap the maximum benefit it is essential to know something of the language before you start, and you would need to ensure that the course is fairly intensive.

There are numerous schools and colleges abroad offering language courses in both the public and private sectors, but it is advisable to make sure that they cater for foreigners, not the nationals of that particular country. For this reason it is sensible to enlist the services of a specialist agency in the United Kingdom such as Euro-Academy Outbound or SIBS, or consult the embassy or cultural institute of the country where you propose to study.

If you are keen to use your vacation to good purpose, a summer language course may be the answer. These normally last for up to a month and are organised by cultural organisations and universities as well as by private schools. Many have the added attraction of being held in delightful locations such as the French Riviera, Florence or Vienna. There are also schemes pioneered by Home Language Lessons where you live and study in your teacher's home.

For details of courses abroad consult *Study Abroad* (UNESCO), *Study Holidays* (Central Bureau for Educational Visits and Exchanges), *Where and How* (Wie und Wo Verlag) or *How to Study Abroad* (How To Books).

The educational advertisement columns of the quality press and *Language Travel Gazette* often contain details of language courses in foreign countries.

Language schools in Britain may have details of courses at affiliated institutions abroad.

HOW TO LIVE & WORK IN SPAIN
Robert A C Richards

Written by a British expatriate who has lived and worked in Spain for for than 25 years, this book provides a user-friendly guide for everyone planning to live in Spain on a temporary or permanent basis, whether for business, professional purposes, study, leisure or retirement. Written with considerable gusto, the book gives a fascinating warts 'n' all account of Spain's variegated lifestyles and how to cope. 'As well as the sort of information one might expect eg work permits, visas, property buying and financial matters, there is so much additional information on health care, travel, holidays, history, geography etc that I feel it would be a good read for the more casual visitor. . . The information is presented in an orderly and interesting way' *Phoenix/Association of Graduate Careers Advisory Services.* Robert A C Richards graduated from London University. Since 1963 he has lived fulltime in Spain, working first as a teacher and now as a foreign press correspondent.

£7.99, 160pp illus. 1 85703 011 7.

Please add postage & packing (UK £1.00 per copy. Europe £2.00 per copy. World £3.00 per copy airmail).
How To Books Ltd, Plymbridge House, Estover Road, Plymouth PL6 7PZ, United Kingdom. Tel: (0752) 695745. Fax: (0752) 695699. Telex: 45635.

4
Getting Down to Language Learning

Everyone experiences a sense of bewilderment at the beginning of a language course, and not without cause. You are casting off into unknown territory, as it were, and this feeling is particularly acute among people who have not learned a language since their schooldays.

Some courses start you off gently with the teacher spending much of the time in the initial stages speaking to you in English. Others are more brutal: they aim to immerse you in the foreign language right from the start, and little, if any, communication takes place in your mother tongue.

Learning a language is rather like learning to swim where you are either led into the water by degrees, or you are pushed in. Each teacher and each textbook writer has his own ideas on the best method to teach a particular language.

Often the methods will suit you down to the ground, and you feel confident that you are setting about things the right way. However, some of the ideas used may seem strange, even pointless, despite the fact that the teacher has a reputation for achieving excellent results.

Teaching techniques can vary considerably. One teacher may use a rather formal style of teaching, keeping closely to the book and demanding precision on the part of his students; another may be quite the opposite, offering loosely structured lessons which involve you in activities that are great fun but seem to have no purpose.

If you experience learning problems, the fault may not lie with the teacher or yourself but with the course materials, which may be unattractive or difficult to follow — though there have been great improvements in this area. The teaching environment may have certain shortcomings as well: uncongenial classrooms, poor acoustics, and oversized classes are all problems which could affect your enjoyment and hamper effective learning.

On the other hand, the problem could be you — the language learner — and your lack of experience in tackling a foreign language. You may not always understand what the teacher is talking about or lose the drift of the lesson. Such people easily become discouraged and often abandon the course.

Yet lack of language learning experience is no crime, and there are ways of overcoming it. I myself am utterly unsophisticated as far as information technology is concerned, yet I have struggled with incomprehensible manuals to get on top of the subject in order to word-process this book, and the novice language learner needs to adopt similar tactics *vis-à-vis* language learning.

This chapter aims to get you off to a good start by looking at some aspects of language learning that you may be unaware of or else deterred by.

The pitfalls of pronunciation: individual sounds

Speaking a foreign language correctly is perhaps the most difficult of all skills. If you are writing the language you have time to think and look up the words you don't know; you also have time for second thoughts and can go through and correct what you have written. By contrast if you are conversing with someone an instant reaction is called for and you have to think on your feet. Not only do you have to put together words in an understandable way; you also have to speak them in an intelligible fashion.

Inappropriate pronunciation is an age-old problem. In *The Canterbury Tales*, for instance, Chaucer mentions a prioress who spoke French. . .

'After the school of Stratford-atte-Bowe,

For the French of Paris was to her unknown'.

If we are going to speak French we ought to make a stab at speaking it as it is spoken in France. Chaucer's prioress suffered from a disadvantage: she had never had an opportunity to hear authentic French accents, and doubtless her teacher would have been in a similar position. We, however, have no such excuse, thanks to cassette recorders, language laboratories and other paraphernalia which enable us to hear French (or indeed any language) as it should be spoken.

Have you ever listened to a foreigner speaking English? The Chinese waiter who serves you with 'fly lice' (fried rice), the Spaniard who orders 'esteak and espinach', the Viennese German lady with the 'vonderful het' or the Frenchman who cannot stand 'zees eengleesh wezzer'. These people are encountering certain problems, which could be easily overcome, if they could only identify the problem and seek to remedy it.

What are the problems for the people just mentioned? In most cases they are being called upon to utter sounds in English which do not exist in their own languages. The Frenchman cited above has problems wiith the two sounds that we designate with the letters 'th' (ð and θ in the International Phonetic Alphabet); and the short 'i' sound (as in 'this') also causes difficulties. German-speakers do not have 'w's like ours at the beginning of words and the nearest they come to an English 'a' (as in hat) is 'e', hence the difficulty of the Viennese lady.

The Spaniard in the restaurant, like most of his compatriots, has difficulty in pronouncing certain clusters of consonants at the beginnings of words and adds an 'e' as he does in his own language — Espagnol. The hapless Chinese has never been in the habit of pronouncing clusters of consonants in his language; and as for consonants at the end of words, these are relatively uncommon in Chinese, so he simply ignores them.

Although I am no dyed-in-the-wool Professor Higgins, I believe it is important to develop good speech habits in the target language right from the outset. Yet some self-conscious learners and teachers neglect this aspect of language. They look on pronunciation exercises as embarrassing, even ludicrous. Athletes and footballers, on the other hand, have no qualms about indulging in much more ludicrous activities in order to become fit.

THE ORGANS OF SPEECH

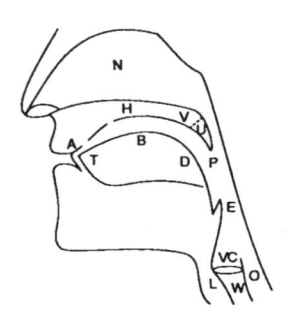

N	Nasal cavity		A	Alveolar ridge
H	Hard palette		V	Soft palette, velum
U	Uvula		T	Tip, apex
B	Blade, front		D	Dorsum, back
P	Pharynx		L	Larynx
VC	Vocal cords		W	Trachea, windpipe
O	Oesophagus, food passage		E	Epiglottis

Getting Down to Language Learning 39

How do you set about improving your pronunciation? It is instructive to note how a child learns to talk: first he listens and watches carefully, then he imitates the sounds he hears. Adult learners need to do the same. If you have difficulty in identifying or imitating a particular sound, you might try to find out how it is articulated. The position of the tongue is particularly important.

Let's now have a look at two sounds in French that English-speakers tend to pronounce wrongly: the 't' and the 'u' sounds. The word 'tu' (meaning 'you') is often pronounced like the word 'two' or 'chew', but that pronunciation is 'after the school of Stratford-atte-Bow', not the real thing at all. What exactly are the problems?

One of them is that in English we are used to aspirating 't' (i.e. releasing it with a puff of breath) when it occurs alone at the beginning of a word, whereas the French do not aspirate their 't'. In the case of the French 'u' sound, there is no equivalent in English.

So how do we solve the first problem? This is not too difficult since we do have an unaspirated 't' in English. If you say 'top' it is aspirated; but if you put another consonant in front of it, as for instance 'stop', it isn't. Try saying 'stop' without the 's' and you are on your way to pronouncing the French 't'.

The French 'u' sound is also attainable quite easily. Say 'i' and purse your lips as if you want to whistle. Alternatively say 'oo' and move your tongue forward. You may not get it right the first time, but if you are aware of what you are doing wrong and know what you are aiming for, you will master the sound. Practice will make perfect.

Don't be too much of a perfectionist at the beginning or you may become tongue-tied — literally! A good language teacher will teach pronunciation with a fairly light touch, since more than five or ten minutes devoted to improving pronunciation can result in tedium.

As you become more adept at languages you may find it worth your while to learn about the International Phonetic Alphabet, which seeks to codify the sounds of every conceivable language.

The pitfalls of pronunciation: the melody of speech

If you listen carefully to someone speaking an unfamiliar language you will notice that it has a certain melody and rhythm. The rise and fall (or intonation) differs from language to language, and is often reproduced even when a foreign person speaks English. We can often tell an Italian, a Spaniard or a Chinese from the melody pattern he applies to our language.

THE INTERNATIONAL PHONETIC ALPHABET

Consonants	Bilabial	Labio-dental	Dental and Alveolar	Retroflex	Palato-alveolar	Alveolo-palatal	Palatal	Velar	Uvular	Pharyngal	Glottal
Plosive	p b		t d	ʈ ɖ			c ɟ	k g	q G		ʔ
Nasal	m	ɱ	n	ɳ			ɲ		ŋ N		
Lateral fricative			ɬ ɮ								
Lateral non-fricative			l	ɭ			ʎ				
Rolled			r						R		
Flapped			ɾ	ʈ					ʀ		
Fricative	ɸ β	f v	θ ð s z ɹ	ʂ ʐ	ʃ ʒ	ɕ ʑ	ç j	x ɣ	χ ʁ	ħ ʕ	h ɦ
Frictionless continuants and semi-vowels	w ɥ	ʋ	ɹ				j (ɥ)	(w)	ʁ		

Vowels						Front	Central	Back			
Close	(y ʉ u)					i y	i ʉ	ɯ u			
Half-close	(ø o)					e ø	ə	ɤ o			
Half-open	(œ ɔ)					ɛ œ	ɜ	ʌ ɔ			
						æ					
Open	(ɒ)					a	ɑ ɒ				

(Secondary articulations are shown by symbols in brackets)

Getting Down to Language Learning

Let's look at a few examples of English intonation to start with. The melody of the sentence 'He's coming' is different from that of 'He's coming?' In the first melody falls at the end of the sentence, while in the second the melody rises. The melody in both cases has a grammatical role to differentiate between a statement and a question.

Intonation also reveals a person's attitude to whoever he is addressing — in English, at least. If you are showing interest in a person or occurrence your speech melody is likely to have much more pitch variation (i.e. rise and fall more) than it would if you were dealing with a fairly mundane matter.

If you hear someone speaking in a monotone, like one of Dr Who's Daleks, he will sound threatening and sinister, and you will dislike his tone of voice — quite literally. By contrast, Welsh people often give the impression of being much more interested in people than the rest of us because of their lilting accent.

We tend to take it for granted that our intonation patterns can be applied to different languages, but it is dangerous to assume this. By adopting the incorrect intonation in a foreign language you could be conveying a misleading impression.

This is perhaps a good place to mention a problem that English-speakers encounter when they come across a tonal language, such as Chinese, Thai, Vietnamese and certain African languages. In these languages by modifying the pitch of a particular vowel you change the meaning of the word.

The Thai language, for instance, has a word that sounds just like the English 'cow'. It means 'news', 'rice', 'he/she/it' or 'white' depending on the pitch you give to the word. If you get the tone wrong you run the risk of saying something dreadful. When complimenting a Thai girl on her good looks, for example, you have to make sure you use the word 'suay' (rising tone) which means 'pretty' and not 'suay' (level tone) which means 'unlucky'.

Another important component of English speech is stress. Most of us are aware that stress is present in English poetry. For example:
'The CURfew TOLLS the KNELL of PARTing DAY,
The LOWing HERD winds SLOWly O'ER the LEA. . .'
HowEVer CERtain SYLLables are ALso STRESSED in NORmal SPEECH. This happens in other Germanic languages (such as German and Dutch) and in the Slavonic languages. But in other languages such as French or Italian stress appears to be virtually absent. If you really want to sound like an Italian you need to cast off your Anglo-Saxon stress patterns.

In English we can also accord importance to particular WORDS in a sentence by the judicious use of stress. For example:

'GORDON bought flowers for Louise' (Gordon did it, not someone else)

'Gordon BOUGHT flowers for Louise' (He didn't pick them)

'Gordon bought FLOWERS for Louise' (Not chocolates)

'Gordon bought flowers for LOUISE' (not Mary)

However, this tradition is not necessarily carried over into other languages. In German you might emphasise a word by putting it in first position in a sentence; in French you would have to add extra words; in other languages you might repeat a particular word to emphasise it.

While some course books may use diagrams and diacritics to demonstrate intonation and stress, the best way to learn is by careful listening and imitation. Your teacher may well ask the class to repeat sentences in chorus, and, although this technique may strike you as redolent of a primary school, it is not a bad way to learn. Rather than sulk at the back of the class you need to join in with gusto. Drills in a language laboratory are another way of learning good speech habits in your target language.

Grappling with grammar

Mention of the word 'grammar' is apt to terrify the faint-hearted, and put them off embarking on a course of foreign language. Yet we all use grammar in our everyday life, normally unconsciously; if we didn't we just wouldn't be able to make ourselves understood. For the purposes of this book I am going to regard grammar as a system of putting words together to make sentences.

Language learners (and some teachers) are wary of grammar because in the past language course writers seemed to regard grammatical rules as the be-all and end-all of language learning. Traditional courses would give you a list of vocabulary and a set of rules and then expect you to translate isolated sentences from one language into another; effective communication seemed far from their minds.

For most learners the ability to communicate in a foreign tongue is far more important than being able to describe how the language works or to conjugate the pluperfect of this or the subjunctive of that. Some language teachers, following the example of Maximilian Berlitz, have therefore reacted against this academic tradition and seek to eliminate grammatical rules from their courses.

Yet most learners welcome brief grammatical explanations after they have been exposed to a sequence of sentences and dialogues.

Without guidance of this nature many people would try to reinvent the wheel and make up rules of their own, which could prove erroneous. Grammar has its uses, notably in pointing out differences in usage between the target language and English.

To begin with, let us consider word order. In English the verb usually comes somewhere near the beginning of the sentence after the subject, while in Japanese it comes at the end. In English the subject usually has to come before the verb except in questions; in German it can come after the verb; while in Welsh the verb always precedes the subject. Once you understand that languages behave differently and start to take note of different rules, you are less likely to make mistakes.

Unfortunately, there aren't rules to cover everything. Certain kinds of words cause particular problems, and prepositions are a case in point. We say 'IN my opinion', the French say 'AT my opinion' (à mon avis) and the Germans say 'my opinion AFTER' (meiner Meinung nach). Rules, alas, are not God-given, and as far as language is concerned it is not possible to make them to cover every eventuality.

Genders and tenses: are they logical?

One idea that English-speakers find somewhat illogical is the way many European languages accord nouns different genders. Thus in German 'Schuh' (shoe) is masculine, 'Glocke' (bell) is feminine, and Mädchen' (girl) is neuter, and when they are preceded by an article it has to be of the correct gender, too — 'ein' or 'eine' in the case of the indefinite article ('a'); 'der', 'die' or 'das' in the case of the definite article ('the'). If an adjective precedes the noun, that has to assume an appropriate form, too.

It all sounds very odd, but we are making the mistake of confusing grammatical gender with biological gender, and these are quite separate concepts. The trouble with languages is that in most cases they have developed over the centuries rather than been formulated by a logical mind (artificial languages, such as Esperanto, are the exception), and so they cannot pretend to be logical. To a foreigner English may appear completely crazy, while his own mother tongue is logic incarnate!

As if gender was not confusing enough, nouns often have special endings according to their function in the sentence. We have this sytem in small measure in English: if you add S or ES to a noun you make it plural (though there are exceptions); if you add apostrophe plus S('S) you make it a possessive. A Turkish noun, on the other hand, has six endings in the singular; for example 'ev' (meaning 'house') can also appear as 'eve', 'evi', 'evde', 'evden' and 'evin' — and we haven't yet started talking about the plural!

Turkish nouns and pronouns, like those in Latin, Russian, Greek, etc., are declined and each ending denotes a particular case: nominative to denote that the noun functions as a subject; genitive to denote that the noun is possessive (e.g. the man's, the children's). Other cases are the dative, ablative, instrumental and locative, but alas they do not function in precisely the same way in every language.

The Chinese, by contrast, have a much happier time: their nouns undergo no modification and do not even have a plural form. Their language has its difficulties, but finding the right suffix is not one of them.

Verbs are perhaps the most difficult item to come to terms with in many languages. One verb can take on a variety of forms. In English the verb 'eat' also appears in different contexts as 'eats', 'ate', 'eaten', 'eating', but a French verb can assume over a hundred different guises depending on the tense and its subject. Learning French verb tables (or Latin, Russian, Greek, Spanish or Italian ones, for that matter) is a chore that kills off many a schoolchild's enthusiasm for languages, but there is no easy way out for a serious learner.

Knowing how to use tenses correctly can be even more of a challenge. Tense systems vary from language to language. For instance: English has two ways of expressing the present tense as in 'I eat' and 'I am eating'; while many other languages only have one. However, European languages strike back by boasting a form that is virtually extinct in English: the subjunctive.

The terminology used can also mislead. Romance and other Germanic languages have perfect tenses just as we do, but they are not necessarily used in the same way. When the French use the perfect tense we would possibly use the past tense ('Je l'ai vu hier soir': 'I saw him last night'); and in certain instances when we use the perfect, the French would use the present tense ('I have been here for five hours': 'Je suis ici depuis cinq heures'). In German the past and perfect tenses are often interchangeable.

So one needs to approach tenses with caution, paying attention to how they are used in context rather than trying to find precise equivalents in English. Not that pouring over grammar manuals will necessarily help you attain fluency. You may well find that it is only through reading passages in your target language and listening to conversations by native speakers that a pattern emerges.

Getting Down to Language Learning

I remember how a friend of mine once spent a summer in France and returned quite adept at using the subjunctive! Your teacher, if he is worth his salt, should be able to give you some guidance if he is made aware of your difficulty.

Words, words, words

If grammar is the mortar of a language vocabulary represents the bricks. But you can't really have one without the other. Some people make the mistake of thinking that the best way to progress in a language is to learn lists of words and become the equivalent of a speaking dictionary. It isn't.

We need to recognise that words vary in importance. There are useful ones which you will use frequently, those that you may need in certain circumstances, and others which you need to understand but are unlikely to use yourself. To put it another way, in English you have an active vocabulary — one that you will use regularly — and a passive vocabulary — words you may come across intermittently in books and newspapers.

There are perhaps 1,000 to 1,500 words that we are constantly using, and often these are the ones that are most difficult to acquire. Once you have acquired them, learning new vocabulary becomes much easier, because you start to perceive relationships with other words in the language or perhaps your own.

If you are learning any European language (with the exception of about five) you will start to notice relationships with English, and it is not surprising. Roughly half of the vocabulary we use in English is derived from Norman French or Latin (Romance languages) while the other half is related to words in other Germanic languages. Since the major languages of Western Europe and the Americas belong to either the Germanic or Romance language group, English-speakers start out with a considerable linguistic advantage over the Japanese or Arabs.

One must not assume that things are always what they seem. With the passage of time some words change their meanings. Thus in French, the word for 'vicar' is 'curé', while the equivalent of 'curate' is 'vicaire' — a point worth remembering if you are not to commit a *faux pas* in French ecclesiastical circles.

When in doubt you can always consult a dictionary, but remember that dictionaries can mislead and you can never rely on finding the precise equivalent of a particular word. French for instance has two words for river, whereas we have only one. If you call the Seine 'une rivière' a French person is likely to be taken aback, for the Seine is 'un fleuve' in French eyes, even though its tributaries certainly can be designated 'rivières'.

German words may look different from English words, but in many cases you can find the English equivalent by changing around the sounds. Thus, if you replace 'd' or 't' in certain words, 'Bad' becomes 'bath', 'Dorn' becomes 'thorn'; interchange 'p' and 'f' and 'Klippe' becomes 'cliff', while 'Pfeife' becomes 'pipe'.

As one moves away from Western European languages there are fewer familiar landmarks to latch on to, which is partly why they take longer to learn. Let us take Japanese as an example. The Japanese words 'jimusho', 'kuruma', 'shimbun' and 'kaban' will bear no resemblance to anything an English-speaker has yet come across, and you may despair of ever learning them, particularly if your memory is no longer what it was.

Fortunately there are a few techniques which will assist your learning. Rather than learn lists of words with their English equivalents (office, car, newspaper, briefcase) in isolation, try to learn them within a context. One idea you might try is to put them together in a sentence like 'My Kaban briefcase is in the Kuruma car and the Shimbun newspaper is in Jim Usho's office'. Try to form a picture in your mind. An alternative would be to learn words in association — a practice known as mnemotechnics. e.g. 'When I rev my car it goes kuruma, kuruma'; 'Jim, you show me my office'. Again you try to form a mental picture to make the words stick in your mind.

I mentioned in the section on grammar that in many languages nouns have genders, and you should always endeavour to learn the gender as well as the spelling and meaning of the noun in question. But do not expect to understand every word a foreigner says or writes. As you become more experienced you will be able to guess at the meaning of words from the context in which they appear.

Writing systems with a difference
There are some 50 distinctive sounds (phonemes) in both English and French speech and only 26 letters to represent them. In some cases the number of letters is increased by the use of diacritics. German, for instance, puts two dots (umlaut) over the vowels a, o and u (ä, ö, ü) in order to modify the sound. Slavonic languages which use the Roman alphabet make use of the ˇ symbol to express the sounds (š and č) which we in English would spell sh and ch. But such differences are easily learned.

The problems start when the language you are learning does not use Roman script — Russian and Greek, for example. Fortunately in the case of both languages there are signs that are familiar. Greek symbols figure quite prominently in mathematics. In Russian some letters are familiar (a, e, o) and others are familiar though representing different sounds (B = v; H = n; P = r; C = s). You have to get used to only a dozen or so letters which are completely new.

If you venture beyond Europe the going gets tougher with alphabets that degenerate into a jumble of incomprehensible hieroglyphics written not only from right to left but also from top to bottom. Writing systems like this seem designed to deter all but the most persistent scholar.

Fortunately there is an easy way out, and it is not retreat! If your principal aim is to speak and understand the spoken language, you are not obliged to get to grips with the script. Other English-speakers have trodden this path before you, and as a consequence there are several courses on the market — for Japanese, Chinese, Arabic, Thai and Cambodian, to name but a few — that do not require you to master a new alphabet at all. In the course of time when you have mastered the rudiments of the spoken language you may well wish to. If you want to look a word up in a dictionary you will need to know the script of the language.

Fortunately mastery of one alphabet can sometimes open doors to other languages. Once you have mastered Arabic writing, for instance, you will also be able to write Persian and Urdu. If you can learn one Indian script, several others will be within your grasp. Chinese represents a particular problem, but once you have learned a certain number of characters, you will discover certain principles are at work and the rest will come more easily.

Conclusion

In this chapter I have highlighted some of the problems that people need to be aware of when learning a language. However, it is worth bearing in mind that all languages are different and you will not necessarily encounter the same problems in one language as you do in another. Chinese and Thai may have formidable scripts, but they don't have nouns that you decline or verbs you have to conjugate. What you lose on the swings you gain on the roundabouts.

As when learning to ride a bike or drive a car, you cannot hope to get everything right first time round. You will make mistakes, many of them quite understandable. One reason is that you are applying rules from your mother tongue; making generalisations about rules in the target language which are wrong; or translating words instead of ideas.

Language learning, alas, is never a completely painless process. At times you will experience mental blocks and feel so discouraged that you contemplate giving the whole enterprise up. However, there is no need to worry yourself unduly. Things have the habit of falling into place. Console yourself with the thought that you have already succeeded in learning one language quite well — namely, your own. With a little persistence you will soon be able to master another.

HOW TO SPEND A YEAR ABROAD
Nick Vandome

A year abroad is now a very popular option among thousands of school leavers, students, and people taking a mid-life break. This book sets out the numerous options available from making the decision to go, to working on a kibbutz, to teaching English as a foreign language, to adapting to life at home on your return. 'Should be required reading... Unlike most reference books this is one which should be ready right through, and that is a pleasure as well as being very informative. It is totally comprehensive... very good value for money.' *The School Librarian*. Nick Vandome is a young freelance writer who has spent a year abroad on three occasions, in France, Australia, Africa and Asia. His articles have appeared in *The Guardian, The Scotsman, The Daily Telegraph*, and elsewhere. He is also the author of *How to Get a Job in Australia* in this series.

£7.99, 176pp illus. 1 85703 046 X.

Please add postage & packing (UK £1.00 per copy. Europe £2.00 per copy. World £3.00 per copy airmail).
How To Books Ltd, Plymbridge House, Estover Road, Plymouth PL6 7PZ, United Kingdom. Tel: (0752) 695745. Fax: (0752) 695699. Telex: 45635.

5
Issues and Problems for the Language Learner

Chapter 4 served as a brief introduction to language learning. However, there are bound to be other questions that will pass through your mind. The following pages therefore offer advice and suggestions on a number of key topics.

APTITUDE AND ABILITY

A great many people believe that they will never become proficient in another language because they have no aptitude for languages. While it is true that some people appear to have a greater facility for languages than others, in the same way that some people are better footballers than others, this does not mean that you shouldn't be able to acquire a foreign tongue provided you are prepared to make an effort.

I fear people are put off learning other languages because in the Anglo-Saxon world linguistic ability has always been associated with intelligence. Thus in Shakespeare's *Twelfth Night* Sir Toby Belch has no doubt in his mind that Sir Andrew Aguecheek is a man of considerable accomplishment. 'He plays o' th' viol-de-gamboys, and speaks three or four languages word for word without book,' he boasts to his niece's chambermaid.

Yet musical ability and the 'gift of tongues' are not beyond the reach of ordinary mortals. Nationals of other countries show no such reticence about mastering another language. If you cross the North Sea, you will find most Dutch people speak at least one foreign language and possibly two or three. Go to Africa and you will find that even the poorly educated street vendors command two or three languages. Visit a primary school in rural Wales and you will find every child is proficient in both Welsh and English.

This situation has come about not because the Dutch, the Africans and the Welsh are cleverer than the rest of us. It is because they are motivated — often by money — and motivation, like love, can overcome everything.

BUSINESS

Business people often see mastery of a foreign language as a means by which they can negotiate million-dollar deals and secure lucrative contracts. So they search for the perfect business course which will enable them to do this in the shortest time possible.

Unfortunately too many expect to run before they can walk. Whatever the language, it is essential to master the basics first of all, and this means learning to string words together to make coherent sentences and getting your pronunciation right. While there are a few excellent language courses with a business bias for the commoner languages designed for complete beginners,* most of them assume that you already have some knowledge of the language.†

This fact should certainly not deter people. Any basic knowledge of a language will be useful whether you land in Tehran or Tokyo. Modern language courses are extremely practical and will enable you to introduce yourself, order a meal, find your way about, and operate within a limited range.

However, until you have reached a fairly advanced level, you will need to rely on the services of a trained interpreter in complex commercial discussions. Nevertheless, with a little effort you should be able to get the drift of the conversation, and your apparent determination to speak their language is likely to make a favourable impression on prospective clients.

CILT produces lists of business oriented materials (books and cassettes) for French, German and Spanish. See also Chapter 7.

COURSE BOOKS

If you register for a course, the decision on course books has usually been made for you. If you opt for self-study you can choose your own learning package which should ideally consist not only of a course book but audio cassettes and perhaps video cassettes as well. Appendix A offers guidance in this area.

Although High Street bookshops often have language courses on their shelves (especially courses that tie in with TV and radio programmes) the best idea is to go to a bookshop with a wide range of courses on offer — academic bookshops, such as Foyles, Dillons, Blackwells, etc., or one of the specialist booksellers

---

*Such as the 'Language for Business' series (Limitcode), 'Working with' series (Stanley Thornes), and Managed Learning courses.
†Such as the multi-media French and German business packages from Pitman.

Issues and Problems for the Language Learner 51

mentioned in Appendix C, such as LCL or Grant & Cutler. Browse through the courses to find one that you feel at ease with.

If you live some distance away from a really good language bookshop, you could send away to publishers or distributors for details of any books that take your fancy. Local libraries, particularly the main branches, also generally have a good selection of book catalogues.

The following questions should help you to decide on the most suitable course:

- Are there cassettes, records or broadcasts to accompany the course?

- Is it an up-to-date course (not a reprint of an old course)?

- Is it well presented and easy to understand?

- Does anyone I know and trust recommend this particular course?

- Is there any indication in the introduction that the course is suitable for self-study?

- Do the aims of the course coincide with my language learning objectives?

If the answer is 'yes' to every question, you can buy with confidence.

For the more widely studied languages there is a huge range of courses. Some of them are single volumes — often accompanied by a cassette — and are basically an introduction to the language; some are clearly designed with tourists in mind and are set out along the lines of a phrase-book; some stretch to two or three volumes and are for people who want to study the language to a reasonably advanced level and perhaps pass an examination; some stress spoken language, while others emphasise reading and writing.

If you are not sure how far you wish to progress with a language, it would be sensible to start off with an inexpensive introductory course, such as the BBC's 'Get by in . . .' series, and perhaps move on to a more elaborate course later. As you become more immersed in the language it will at some stage doubtless become necessary to engage the services of a tutor or enrol for a class in order to get conversational practice.

Incidentally, I have to admit that not all the course books I mention in Appendix A are easy to learn from. For many of the less commonly taught languages the choice of materials is limited and the learner has to make do with whatever is available.

DIFFERENCES IN APPROACH

Which is the best way to learn a foreign language? Unfortunately, it is impossible to give a succinct answer. The fact is that people learn differently. One person may prefer to be taught using the so-called Direct Method where there is no recourse to the learner's mother tongue; another may learn more effectively if the different language points are explained. Some like to hear sentences before they attempt to speak them, while others need to see them first in black and white.

Another consideration is that languages differ too, and a learning strategy that works well for one language may fail if you tackle a completely different one. You may, for example, be able to guess the meanings of words in Western European languages, while the vocabulary of Japanese or Arabic may seem very exotic and remote.

A few years ago the American educationist Earl Stevick[*] investigated the learning strategies of seven people who had mastered a language successfully, and discovered a considerable variation in approach. One, whom he characterises as an intuitive learner, had the knack of acquiring the language subconsciously, while a second benefited from a more formal approach with massive repetition and memorising of dialogues.

Another of his informants managed to pick up the target language in an informal manner, though at the expense of grammatical accuracy, while a fourth applied his imagination to the language learning task. A fifth learner adopted an active approach and built on his linguistic strengths, while a sixth, described as a 'deliberate learner', put her whole self into the language learning process, practising the language at every spare moment. The seventh, the 'self-aware learner', adopted an intellectual approach to her language learning.

The moral of the investigation is that there is no one golden method of learning a foreign language. The language learner should opt for the learning strategy he feels most comfortable with, no matter what others think or do.

---

[*]Stevick, E. W.: *Success with Foreign Languages* (Prentice Hall International, 66 Wood Lane, Hemel Hempstead HP2 4RG).

EMBARRASSMENT

Some people are afraid to open their mouths for fear they will make a mistake and look foolish. However, such fears are out of place in a well-organised adult language class where the atmosphere ought to be relaxed rather than forbidding. Indeed, there is a school of thought that suggests that people cannot learn languages effectively unless they are completely relaxed.*

While language schools generally go out of their way to provide a pleasant atmosphere, in many public-sector institutions language courses are held in multi-purpose classrooms where the seating arrangements are more appropriate to formal lectures than informal intercourse. Such classroom situations may bring back memories of one's school-days where you were given a black mark for a wrong answer.

I often feel that the best venue for a language course would be a pub since course members would be much more likely to cast off their inhibitions in this kind of environment. The fact is that it doesn't matter two hoots whether you make mistakes provided that you learn from them. Concentrate on your language learning rather than on your perceived inadequacies, and you will not have a chance to feel embarrassed.

The same is true when you are speaking to foreigners in their own language. There is absolutely no need to feel shy or be hesitant; they will be delighted that you are making the effort to address them in their own language and will forgive you any mistakes you make.

Problems may arise in special in-house company language courses because of the composition of the class. There may be course members who are subordinate to you, so that you feel obliged to perform better than they do. This is a good reason for joining a class where your classmates are complete strangers. (See also Chapter 7.)

FREQUENCY OF LEARNING

If your language class meets but once a week, you will doubtless find that you forget a good deal in the intervening seven days. Alas, one's memory is a fickle companion, which discards an alarming amount of useful data in the first 24 hours after it has been acquired.

---

*Rose, C.: *Accelerated Learning* (Accelerated Learning Systems Ltd., 50 Aylesbury Road, Aston Clinton, Aylesbury, Bucks).

In order to maintain the language level you have attained and move forward from it, you need regular and frequent practice. Such practice need not entail a great deal of time. One course I came across when compiling this book was entitled 'Spanish for 10 minutes a day' and was based on the principle that 'short and frequent' is better than 'long and seldom'.

Instead of opting for a once-a-week course, see if you can enrol for one which meets more frequently, expecially in the early stages of the language when you need all the 'thrust' you can get in order to take off successfully. Best of all, find a course which is held every day. You will then make quicker progress, and the learning will come easier.

If such an arrangement is impossible, you should at least endeavour to practise the target language yourself. Every day you need to review the last lesson you did and prepare for the next; you might also listen to language cassettes as you drive to work or practise dialogues with yourself in the bath. Whenever you have a spare moment, practise, practise, practise.

GESTURE

Human beings communicate not only with their voice but with other parts of their body as well — with their hands, their face, their head, their shoulders. This has important implications for the language learner. For instance, if you are ever lost for words, you can usually resort to gesture rather than having to fall back on your own language.

One idea that may act as a fillip to your language learning is that you should endeavour not merely to sound like a native speaker of your target language, but also try to act like one. When you are speaking Italian do not hesitate to use your hands; when speaking French try to use French facial expressions.

I have known many quiet, unassuming people who change completely when they appear on the stage in an amateur theatre production. By following their example and assuming a new persona in the language class you may well find that you become much more articulate.

HANDICAPS

'I don't have an ear for languages.' 'I'm tone deaf.' 'I have a bad memory.' Some people are deterred from taking up a foreign language because they imagine they suffer from all manner of handicaps. Yet most handicaps, whether real or imaginary, can easily be overcome with an ounce of determination.

If you happen to be slightly deaf, just apply the techniques that you use when following speakers of your own language: you watch carefully how they articulate. As for being tone-deaf, that is only a problem if you have ambitions to become an opera singer: there is no relationship whatsoever between musical ability and linguistic ability. Memories only deteriorate as a result of lack of use. (See also 'Words, words, words' in Chapter 4 (page 45).)

It is no handicap to have been bottom of the class in languages at school or never to have learned a foreign language in your life. The older you get the wiser you become, and, if you can approach the task of language learning without preconceptions about yourself, it could prove an advantage.

INTENSIVE COURSES

Intensive courses, by which I mean courses of between roughly 15 and 50 hours' tuition a week, are ideal for anyone who has to learn a language in a hurry. In one month it is possible to learn as much as you could in a year or more on a more conventional type of course.

This type of course may seem expensive, particularly if it involves individual (one-to-one) tuition in an exotic language. Participants on longer courses therefore tend to be either supported by their employers or students in full-time education. Employees about to embark on foreign assignments are sometimes sent on such courses before their departure.

It has to be admitted that intensive courses can be very demanding both physically and mentally, particularly for people who have been out of full-time education for some while and are starting a language from scratch. If it is just a matter of a short course to brush up your language skills, the task is a less arduous one.

The more intensive the course the more varied the learning methods need to be in order to maintain interest. Ideally class teaching should be interspersed with self-study periods, language laboratory sessions, video sessions, interactive learning with computers, and so on. Even the most highly motivated language learner finds his attention wandering during the class and needs a change of activity.

There is much to be said for attending a residential course where you have the chance to practise the language in informal situations when classes are over. Courses held in a country where the target language is spoken are an even better idea.

A number of the organisations listed in Appendix C organise intensive courses, some on a regular basis, others on request. See also Chapters 3 and 7.

JOBS USING LANGUAGES

People often see competence in a foreign language as a means of advancing their careers (see Chapter 1). In some cases language skills are useful: in deciphering letters from foreign clients, for instance. In others they are essential: meeting foreign clients and attending seminars in foreign countries. Increasingly, people need to have a number of foreign languages at their disposal rather than just one.

There are certain people who clearly require competence in other languages, and these include air stewards and stewardesses, conference interpreters and international telephone operators. Yet today any job which involves working in an international sphere is going to require foreign language skills, whether it is working for an international organisation (such as the United Nations or the European Commission), participating in international conferences and research projects, or travelling to foreign countries for research or business.

This is a vast subject and those who wish to pursue it further should consult the following books:

Firth, R. A., Dane, M. and Harris, J. M.: *Your Degree in Modern Languages — What next?* (Association of Graduate Careers Advisory Services).

King. A. and Thomas, G.: *Languages and Careers — An Information Pack* (Centre for Information on Language Teaching and Research — CILT).

Working in Languages (Careers and Occupational Information Centre).

Steadman, H.: *Careers Using Languages* (Kogan Page).

KEEPING UP

'There's no point in me joining a language class. I wouldn't be able to keep up with the others.'

People shy away from language courses because they underestimate their own abilities and overestimate the abilities of others. Admittedly some people have a greater facility for learning

Issues and Problems for the Language Learner

languages than others, but that is no reason why you should fall behind.

There are several ways of ensuring that you keep up:

- Don't miss classes. One of the main reasons why people fall behind and may ultimately drop out of the course is because they do not attend classes regularly.

- Do your homework. Don't just rely on attendance at class to help you learn the language: review your lessons on a regular basis between class meetings.

- Keep ahead in the book. Always spend time before your next class looking over the material you expect to cover. Note down points which you feel might cause you difficulty.

- See if you can transfer to a less advanced class. This is the final resort. It is possible that you have not been placed in a class appropriate to your level. Talk the matter over with your teacher to see what he advises.

Keeping up is a particular problem with intensive courses, since there is little or no opportunity to catch up between classes. There may well be the possibility of transferring to a course that proceeds at a gentler pace, but it is sensible to take advice before you do so.

Bear in mind that if you are struggling at a particular point in a course this may be just a temporary phenomenon, and eventually everything will fall into place. Do not regard yourself as necessarily the best judge of your ability: people have a nasty habit of underestimating themselves.

LEVELS OF COMPETENCE

If you are planning to follow a language course it is important — certainly for your teacher — to know what level of competence in the language you have already attained, what level you are aiming for and what level you would realistically be able to achieve in a given period.

Clearly if you want to learn Albanian and have never learned the language before, there is no problem in deciding where to start from: you begin at the beginning. The complications start with languages such as French or Spanish, which you may have studied and even passed an examination in some time ago. While you may feel you have forgotten the language and would like to start all over again, this is not always the best plan. You are not an absolute beginner and once the course starts you will make rapid progress compared with someone who is a newcomer to the language.

If they (and you) are not sure of your starting level, language training institutes will probably ask you about the books you have studied and the examinations you have taken. They may also ask you to take a short placement test to decide which class to slot you into. From the results they should be able to assess how long it will take you to reach the desired level of competence or examination standard.

What is the difference between advanced and intermediate level, between elementary and advanced? The LCCI chart on pages **60** and **61** describes these terms in everyday language. A feature of this particular scale is that it includes Threshold Level.[*] This — together with the more advanced Waystage — is an internationally recognised specification of language proficiency developed by the Modern Languages Project of the Council of Europe.

You may decide later on to enter for an examination which shows what level of competence you have achieved. The Royal Society of Arts, for instance, offers a Certificate of Language Competence at five levels: Basic, Survival, Threshold, Operational and Advanced.

RSA CERTIFICATE IN LANGUAGE COMPETENCE

Basic
Tests dealing with visitors to a company; arriving at a hotel; entertaining clients; shopping; dealing with directions and signs; travelling on business; making business telephone calls.

Survival
(Equates to Level 1 of the Languages Lead Body standards). Tests listening; reading; conversing socially; doing business by telephone; writing.

Threshold
(Equates to Level 2 of the Languages Lead Body standards.) Tests listening; reading; doing business by telephone; exchanging opinions; conversing formally; writing.

---

[*]Also known as 'U Niveau Seuil', 'Die Kontaktschwelle', 'Livello Soglia' and 'Un Nivel Umbral'. The full specification is set out in *The Threshold Level in a European Unit/Credit System for Modern Language Learning by Adults* by J. A. van Ek (Council of Europe, 1975).

Issues and Problems for the Language Learner 59

Operational
(Equates to Level 3 of the Languages Lead Body standards; suitable for those who have passed GCSE.) Tests listening; reading; doing business by telephone; exchanging opinions, delivering prepared presentation; writing.

Advanced
(Equates to Level 4 of the Languages Lead Body standards; suitable for those who have reached A-Level standard.) Tests listening; reading; discussing products or services; delivering prepared presentation; writing.

MATURE LEARNERS

'I'm too old to start learning a new language.' This kind of remark is more of an excuse than a statement of fact, and stems from the fallacy that the young are much better at picking up languages than their elders. Having come across young people with five years of French behind them who can barely form a sentence in that language, I am not convinced they are.

In these more enlightened times learning is viewed as a lifelong process rather than an activity that is confined to the years of one's youth. The era of the middle-aged student has dawned, and it is not unusual to hear of people in their fifties and sixties who have successfully completed Open University courses. A current language course brochure boasts that it can place anyone between 8 and 80 — and why not?

Young people may have more energy than older ones and they may appear brighter, but while your physical prowess may start to diminish the moment that you pass 30 (or 25) the same cannot be said of your mental powers. Indeed, as far as intellect is concerned an older person possesses a number of advantages:

- His learning span is greater; he can concentrate for longer.

- He has more extensive experience which he can bring to his learning.

- He is usually more highly motivated since he is probably learning for some good reason.

LONDON CHAMBER OF COMMERCE AND INDUSTRY EXAMINATIONS BOARD
PROFILE OF BEHAVIOUR THAT CAN BE EXPECTED FROM FLIC/SEFIC CERTIFICATE HOLDERS AT EACH LEVEL

FLIC/SEFIC LEVEL	FLIC/SEFIC GRADING		BEHAVIOURAL PROFILE	ESU FRAMEWORK SCALE
Limited User	Pass / Credit / Distinction	PRELIMINARY	Successful candidates will be able to "survive" in the language, ie to communicate well enough to secure the daily requirements of a traveller or tourist. They may have a heavy accent, slow delivery and make frequent mistakes, which will make demands on the patience of a listener. They will not dry up, however, but persist until a message is clearly put across and a response is forthcoming.	3
Modest User	Pass / Credit / Distinction	THRESHOLD	Successful candidates will be able to converse adequately though perhaps hesitantly for most social and practical purposes of a routine kind. Though without a specialist business vocabulary, they can nonetheless handle everyday situations at work and make social contacts when abroad, or assist foreign visitors to their own country. Their speech, though not necessarily either fluent or accurate, enables them to communicate on everyday matters, face to face rather than on the telephone.	4 5

Issues and Problems for the Language Learner

FLIC/SEFIC LEVEL	FLIC/SEFIC GRADING		BEHAVIOURAL PROFILE	ESU FRAMEWORK SCALE
Competent User	Pass	INTERMEDIATE	Successful candidates will communicate efficiently at a level sufficient to cope with everyday social and business demands, both direct and on the telephone. They can participate in meetings and report proceedings but still require conscious effort to talk and listen in situations that are not straightforward or are slightly specialised. However, despite making mistakes and missing something of what is said, they will have all the language necessary to offset these defects by enquiring, repeating or rephrasing.	6
	Credit			
	Distinction			
Very Good User	Pass	ADVANCED	Successful candidates will be able to converse fluently, easily and interestingly in the language and to hold the attention of fellow professionals in a range of special topics relating to work. They will be able to discuss, negotiate, present and argue with little diminution of personality, performing comfortably and reliably the oral tasks of business and social life. They will have the range, knowledge and assurance to conduct themselves almost like native speakers.	7
	Credit			
	Distinction			8

The main problem with older people is that they tend to be too self-critical, and underestimate their abilities. Some may experience difficulties with intensive courses, but this is not due to lack of brainpower, but simply to lack of habit. Young people just out of school or college are used to full-time learning, while older people in work aren't. However, that does not mean that you cannot pick up the study habit again; it is just rather painful making the adjustment.

For retired people the following book may be of assistance: *Older Learners — The Challenge of Adult Education* (Help the Aged, PO Box 460, St James's Walk, London WC1R OBE. Tel: (071) 253 0253). Also investigate the University of the Third Age (see Appendix C) to see if it organises language courses in your area.

NEW TECHNOLOGY

'We live in a technological age where machines seem to be taking over. Does that mean that languages will one day be taught by robots?'

This is no idle question. Language learning has changed considerably over the years. First came language records; then tapes which had the advantage that you could stop them and replay passages you did not understand the first time round; and now there are cassette recorders, language laboratories and mini-labs where you can listen to your own voice and compare your answers with the correct ones. Computers are starting to be used in language teaching, and language videos are breaking new ground.

So does that mean that the prospective language learner should seek out the language centre that appears to have the most hi-tech hardware? Not necessarily. Language learning is still very much a person-to-person business and it is the quality of the teaching rather than the excellence of the technology which makes for a successful course.

Audio cassettes offer useful support if you are studying on your own and have the advantage of being relatively cheap. Language videos are more expensive, and, while it may make sense for institutions to acquire them to supplement their language training, the individual purchaser needs to weigh up the cost against the benefit.

The same applies with respect to computer software for language learning. The products available are seldom stand-alone language courses and they also vary considerably in content and quality. It is therefore vital to take advice — from a language trainer, not a

Issues and Problems for the Language Learner

software writer — before buying to ensure that the material really will be of use to you.

A relatively new development is interactive video learning, notably the language courses developed by Vektor, the BBC and IBM laser discs (available from The Learning Centre, Oatby). While these courses may be of interest to language training institutions — especially for their open access courses — they are prohibitively expensive for the individual language learner. Philips are now producing interactive management training programmes on compact discs (CD-Is) which integrate animation, text, graphics, pictures, audio and video. It seems only a matter of time before language courses are developed for this system which uses special compact disc players that can also play conventional CDs.

Bear in mind also that, while the major languages may be well supported with software and other aids, the range of materials (hi-tech or low-tech) for less popular languages is very restricted.

See also Chapter 7.

OPPORTUNITIES

'I don't have opportunity to use my foreign languages. What can I do?'

Languages are meant to be used, and if you do not use them you will become rusty; hence the need to make an effort to find opportunities to practise your language skills.

The ideal solution is to make regular visits to countries where the language is spoken, which is particularly easy if your modern languages are European ones and you happen to live in the British Isles. You might also consider enrolling for a summer course (see Chapter 3).

A number of cities have French, German, Spanish or Italian clubs where you can practise your languages; colleges and university extra-mural departments often offer advanced conversation classes in the commoner languages. To practise some of the less common languages you might visit the meeting-places of émigré associations.

It is quite possible that there are foreign students in your area who speak the languages you are interested in. If such is the case, why not befriend some of them and offer them hospitality?

Most larger public libraries have foreign language books you can borrow, and some — such as the City Business Library, 1 Brewers Hall Garden, London EC3N 1DD — have foreign journals for perusal. Some of the larger newsagents in larger cities sell foreign newspapers, but, if you do not have access to these, you might consider taking out a subscription to a weekly journal such as *L'Express* or *Der Spiegel*.

If you have appropriate equipment, you could tune into foreign radio broadcasts. The *World Radio TV Handbook* (Billboard Books, 1515 Broadway, New York NY 10036), *Dial-Search* (G. Wilcox, 9 Thurrock Close, Eastbourne BN20 9FN. Tel: (0321) 22419 and *International Radio Station Guide* (Bernard Babani, The Grampians, Shepherds Bush Road, London W6 7NF. Tel: (071) 603 2581) provide details of frequencies. Moreover, with the help of a satellite dish aerial it is possible to pick up foreign television transmissions.

For details of courses abroad consult *Study Abroad* (UNESCO): *Study Holidays* (Central Bureau for Educational Visits and Exchanges); *Where and How?* (Wie und Wo Verlag).

For details of language clubs in your locality contact your local reference library. Some of the organisations listed in Appendix C may also have suggestions. See also under 'Visits abroad' (page **68**).

PERSISTENCE

Learning a language is not a straightforward process. You will experience learning peaks and troughs, and the latter can be extremely discouraging. At times you have the impression that you are going into reverse and you chastise yourself for making stupid mistakes. On other occasions you find yourself up against a mental block, where you seem unable to grasp new concepts or absorb any more information; you feel you have reached a plateau and can go no further.

This is a problem that virtually every language learner has to contend with, and it is particularly true of intensive courses. At the end of the day's course the learner sometimes feels completely drained and his brain seems to stop functioning. Does this mean you have reached the end of the road?

Not a bit of it. Look on the brain as a computer that needs to switch off from time to time in order to reassemble the data it has absorbed into a more coherent form. You may have noticed that if you sleep on a particular problem you may well find that by the morning it has been solved.

When things seem to be going from bad to worse the last thing to do is give up. You simply have to persist and take heart from one of the language learners Earl Stevick interviewed who claims: 'I learn more on the days when I'm really tired and beat down.' (See 'Differences in approach' (page **52**).)

Don't get discouraged. Keep bashing on and eventually everything will sort itself out.

QUALIFICATIONS

Not everybody embarks on a language course in the expectation of obtaining a qualification at the end of it all. Indeed, examination-oriented courses are regarded, rightly or wrongly, as less pleasurable than those that are not.

Nevertheless, some language learners like to have a target to aim for, a measure against which their progress can be judged. They may well be looking to the future: a language qualification would doubtless impress a prospective employer and could lead to promotion.

In the United Kingdom most people equate qualifications with GCSE and 'Advanced Level' examinations. Yet there are a number of other language examinations that may be more appropriate to your needs. The Royal Society of Arts, for instance, offers an examination in French, Spanish and German; the London Chamber of Commerce and Industry (LCCI) organises oral examinations at three or four levels for a wide range of foreign languages; and the Institute of Linguists is also active in the field, having introduced their ELIC range (Examinations for International Communication). Languages can also form part of Business and Technician Education Council (BTEC) certificate and diploma course.

For people who prefer a certificate based on assessment rather than performance in an examination, the new Foreign Languages at Work Scheme (FLAW) deserves investigation. This flexible scheme is run by the LCCI in conjunction with the British Overseas Trade Board.

If you attend classes at a foreign cultural centre, you may have the opportunity to take one of their internationally recognised examinations. A number of training organisations issue their own certificates of competence which generally include a written assessment rather than a grade.

If you are taking a course which does not lead to a qualification, and you would like to take an examination, ask your teacher or adviser whether he thinks you are up to the standard of any public examination. If the answer is positive, you can contact an examination board and make your own arrangements to take the examination. If you have in mind an exam which consists mainly of written papers you might consider enrolling for a correspondence course.

READING

Every serious language learner needs to be an avid reader. It is through reading that you extend your vocabulary, particularly your passive vocabulary — the words you need to know but will use only infrequently. Moreover, reading is the most accessible language activity; you can dip into a book in a train, on an aeroplane or while you are waiting for a bus.

Of the four language skills — listening, speaking, reading and writing — reading is the one which you will probably master the quickest. It has the advantage that you can take your time over it, referring to a dictionary as and when necessary, and you can often guess the meaning of a word from its context.

While you cannot expect to read newspapers or *War and Peace* in the original after your first few weeks into the language, you should be able to tackle simplified texts designed for language learners where the vocabulary is restricted to the commoner words. Your teacher should be able to recommend suitable material.

Eventually you might move on to newspapers and magazines, picking out the words you recognise and trying to work out the meaning of the headlines or odd sentences. You do not need to understand every word. It is enough just to get the gist. If you find it helpful, try reading bits of the text aloud.

If your target language is written in an unfamiliar script, you clearly have an obstacle to surmount, particularly if you have been following a spoken course where the words have been transcribed into Roman script. If you are committed to the language for the long term you will find it beneficial to make the effort to master the writing system.

SUCCESS

Earlier in this chapter I pointed out that there is no one road to attaining fluency in a foreign language; each learner is different. But attempts have been made to indicate the features that characterise the successful language learner, and the following ideas formulated by Alice Omaggio[*] may be of assistance. According to Ms Omaggio, successful learners have insight into their own learning styles and preferences.

---

[*] Omaggio, A.: 'Characteristics of successful language learners' (*ERIC/CLL News Bulletin* (May 1978), 118 22nd Street NW, Washington DC 20037).

- take an active approach to the learning task
- are willing to take risks
- are good guessers
- watch not only what words and sentences mean but also how they are put together
- make the new language into a separate system and try to think in it as soon as possible
- are tolerant and outgoing in their approach to the new language.

If there is one word which characterises each of these points it is 'involvement'. A passive stance will not get you very far, and the more actively involved you are in the language learning process the more successful you will be.

TEACHERS

Are women better teachers than men? It is better to be taught by a native speaker of the language? Is it better to have a private tutor or to learn with a group? The answer to all three questions is 'Maybe' ... or 'Maybe not.'

Women language teachers are certainly more numerous than men, but this is not due to superior ability, but simply because more girls than boys study languages at school. A qualified and competent teacher is a qualified and competent teacher regardless of sex. Personality is also important.

You should look for teaching competence in a native speaker, too, and beware of foreigners who approach you with the suggestion that if you teach them English they will instruct you in their tongue. Such arrangements are rarely satisfactory, and very soon you will realise it is a case of the blind leading the blind. Once you become proficient in the language and are in a position to direct your learning it might be a different story.

Being tutored on a one-to-one basis is a very effective way of learning, and demands considerable concentration on the part of both teacher and learner. However, it is not the ideal solution in every case; many people find learning with a group more stimulating because you have a number of personalities interacting instead of just two.

Finally, if you are in a position to choose your own tutor, do not be seduced by charm and good looks. The mark of a good teacher is how effective his teaching is, not how enjoyable his lessons are.

UNDERSTANDING FOREIGNERS

When you start to apply the language skills you have accumulated over months, perhaps years, you could be in for a dreadful shock. You arrive in Italy, say, and attempt to hold a conversation with a local, and he launches forth into a torrent of incomprehensible prose which bears no resemblance to what you have come across on your Italian course. What has gone wrong?

The simple answer is that no language course book can deal with the many varieties of language you are likely to encounter. Instead it concentrates on the standard language of the country, the type of language you will hear on the radio and TV. In a similar way English courses for foreign students will tend to use 'BBC English' rather than 'Geordie' or 'Cockney'.

There is no need to panic. Just as an English ear becomes attuned to a Scots accent, and an American ear to an Australian, so you will begin to make sense of the language of the country you are visiting — in this case, Italy. If your Italian local realises you are a foreigner, he will probably either speak more slowly or use an accent which is closer to the national norm. If he doesn't, take it as a compliment: your Italian is obviously good enough to convince him that you are a compatriot, but from another part of Italy.

Bear in mind that people modify their language according to circumstances: they may use the standard language with strangers and lapse into a more familiar style with friends. This can involve both a shift in accent and vocabulary. It is difficult to learn these concepts adequately in the classroom; you have to observe them for yourself.

VISITS ABROAD

It is not much fun learning a language in limbo: you have to put it in a context. So it is vital to get among people who speak it and practise what you have learned; otherwise you will continue to speak the 'textbook' language.

You may be in the happy position of working for a company or organisation that actually pays you to go abroad on its behalf. If not, you will have to content yourself with a vacation visit. Younger

Issues and Problems for the Language Learner 69

people are in a more fortunate position, since they may be able to participate on an educational exchange (see Chapter 6).

Although package tours often represent good value, they are not always appropriate for the language learner. You may find yourself for most of the time in the company of English-speakers and have little contact with the local populace. To make the most of your visit you need to travel independently. There is much to be said, too, for avoiding the main international tourist centres and heading for places where foreign visitors are few and far between.

If you are left to your own devices you will learn more. You can make the most of your stay by using public transport, making your own hotel arrangements, ordering your own food in restaurants, making visits to the theatre, going to church, participating in festivals, etc. Upsets may occur, but that should not deter you. Think of the language practice you will have sorting out the problems.

One sensible idea is to stay with a family. If you have no foreign contacts, there are a number of hospitality schemes in operation.

When travelling abroad, make sure that you take with you a good phrase-book where vocabulary and sentences are arranged according to situations (e.g. at the station, in a restaurant, etc.). Some of them also include useful tips for the foreign traveller. A selection of phrase-books appears under each language entry in Appendix A.

The book *Home from Home* (Central Bureau for Educational Visits and Exchanges) lists a number of organisations which offer home-stays on a reciprocal basis, and a number of national tourist offices have details of such schemes. One organisation that arranges home-stays on a non-reciprocal basis is International Links.

WORKING ABROAD

The idea of working in a foreign country in order to learn the language has considerable appeal, particularly to the young and impecunious. Working with the local people is indeed an excellent way of learning their language and getting to know their traditions.

For younger people who fancy the idea of temporary work during the vacation, *Working Holidays* (Central Bureau for Educational Visits and Exchanges) should offer some useful ideas, as do the jobs bulletins of Vacation Work International (9 Park End Street, Oxford OX1 1GJ. Tel: (0865) 241978). You should, however, exercise care in your choice of job; you are more likely to practise the language if you are the sole English-speaker on the premises than if you are one of a number of English-speakers at an international work camp.

Older people may find useful suggestions in my own book, *How to Get a Job Abroad* (How To Books) or the various Vacation Work directories.

X FOR EXPENDITURE

How much does it cost to learn a foreign language?

Much depends on how much you are prepared to pay. The starting price is around £10, which should buy an introductory course and a cassette for self-study. If you want a more elaborate self-study course you can spend several hundred pounds.

A standard adult education language course will cost around £50 a term on the basis of one meeting a week. Generally speaking, the greater the number of hours, the greater the cost. Intensive residential weekend courses will cost in the region of £75 to £100. Fees may be reduced or even waived for individuals in certain categories (e.g. students, pensioners).

Language schools tend to charge more; and the more prestigious the name and location the higher the cost. A small language school might charge from around £3 per course hour, the price depending on the size of the class. Individual tuition is expensive: a private tutor would cost you at least £15 an hour; and individual tuition at a language school would work out at between £20 and £30 per hour or more depending on the language. In-house language training courses would cost between £25 and £55 per tutor hour.

An intensive language course would set you back between £50 and £250 a week depending on the level of intensity and the number of students per class. The typical residential course would cost perhaps 50 per cent more.

Courses abroad vary in cost according to the country. The cheapest package (tuition with accommodation) would be around £130 per week. A really deluxe executive course with individual tuition could cost as much as £2,000; but usually it is the company that foots the bill, not the executive himself. Do not forget to add the cost of travel to your destination.

YOUNG PEOPLE AND LANGUAGES

One of the advantages of being young is that your language learning need not cost you a penny, if you are in full-time education. Even if you are not, your employer may be willing to pay

Issues and Problems for the Language Learner 71

for you to attend a language course. There are also scholarships and awards available if you are prepared to look for them. *The Grants Directory* (Macmillan) is a useful guide.

You also have time on your hands — time to spend abroad getting to grips with a particular language or to do a full-time course at college or university. Apart from traditional language courses which focus almost entirely on the language and literature of a particular country, there are combined studies courses where you may study languages in conjunction with marketing or business studies. Many such courses involve a period of residence aboard.

Opportunities may arise to participate on exchange schemes, as companies and organisations seek to foster links with their counterparts abroad. The European Commission is actively involved in promoting such exchanges under a number of initiatives, one of which is called ERASMUS. The Central Bureau of Educational Visits and Exchanges has details of many of these schemes.

Further reading: King, A.: *Degrees of Fluency — A Sixth Former's Guide to Language Degree Courses* (Centre for Information on Language Teaching and Research — CILT).

Hantrais, L.: *The Undergraduate's Guide to Studying Languages* (Centre for Information on Language Teaching and Research — CILT).

Vacation Traineeships for Students (Vacation Work Publications).

ZEAL

This is an excellent key word with which to finish this chapter. Zeal, motivation, enthusiasm (call it what you will) is an ingredient you need in abundance if you are to attain your language objectives.

We all know the old saying, 'You can take a horse to water but you can't make him drink.' Learning is just like that, and it is frustrating to hear of young people at school who have no interest in what they are studying and consequently get nowhere. An enthusiastic adult learner can run rings round an unmotivated pupil.

Your own brand of enthusiasm will buoy you up when the lessons start to drag or your brain begins to addle. If used constructively, it will give you the impetus to see the course through to the end. It will be the crucial factor in ensuring that nothing is allowed to get in the way of your studies.

Zeal is infectious. If you share your enthusiasm with your fellow course members and teacher, even the dullest topic can be transformed into a stimulating experience.

HOW TO GET A JOB IN EUROPE
Mark Hempshell

For a long time, continental Europe was not such a popular place for Britons to live and work. NOW ALL THAT HAS CHANGED. The Single European Market and Europe's rise as the world's leading economic unit, has made it *the* place to get a job. This new **How To** book is the first to set out exactly what opportunities exist in Europe. It contains step-by-step guidance on how to find the vacancies, how to apply, and how to understand and adapt to the cultural and legal framework. Packed throughout with key contacts, sample documents and much hard-to-find information, this book will be an absolutely essential starting point for everyone job-hunting in Europe, whether as a school or college leaver, graduate trainee, technician or professional — and indeed anyone wanting to live and work as a European whether for just a summer vacation or on a more permanent basis.

£8.99, 160pp illus. 1 85703 060 5.

Please add postage & packing (UK £1.00 per copy. Europe £2.00 per copy. World £3.00 per copy airmail).
How To Books Ltd, Plymbridge House, Estover Road, Plymouth PL6 7PZ, United Kingdom. Tel: (0752) 695745. Fax: (0752) 695699. Telex: 45635.

6
Children and Language Learning

Parents who have neither the time nor the need to learn a language themselves often adopt a different stance with regard to their children. They feel that a monolingual child will find himself at a disadvantage in the jobs market of the future, when executives will be operating increasingly in an international context. Hence there is a desire to ensure that their offspring are acquainted with at least one foreign tongue.

In Britain, after years of decline in modern language teaching, the Government is taking steps to promote languages in schools. The new National Curriculum makes provision for every pupil to learn a foreign language at secondary level, as is the practice in most countries in the world.

Unfortunately, this move has come at a time when there is a shortage of qualified language teachers in Britain's state schools, particularly in inner city areas. One hears stories of pupils being taught languages by teachers who do not even have 'O' Level in the language that they are teaching. It is no wonder that their language classes are dull and unimaginative.

Before you enrol your child in a particular school — and this applies in both the state and private sectors — it is vital to enquire about the provision for teaching modern languages — notably, which languages are taught and at what stage in a pupil's career.

FINDING THE RIGHT SCHOOL

The first step is to ask around. Track down parents whose children attend the school you have in mind, ask them how satisfied they are with the progress their sons and daughters are making in languages, and ask to see samples of their children's work, if possible.

You might also ascertain how many pupils take public examinations (e.g. GCSE and 'A' Level) in modern languages and the success rate. The greater the number, the more likely it is that modern languages are taken seriously, accorded high priority and taught well. Also find out whether language tuition stops if your child opts to study science subjects later on in his school career.

Many schools arrange open evenings or open days for prospective parents, which you should endeavour to attend. Introduce yourself to the head of modern languages and find out how many qualified staff and/or native speakers of the languages in question he has at his disposal. If the department seems to be under strength, there is a risk that some classes are taught by unqualified staff.

It might be useful to enquire about the teaching techniques employed. You might ask the following questions:

- Are lessons all 'chalk and talk' or do the teachers have access to audio-visual aids that are used on a regular basis?

- How much emphasis is put on listening and speaking?

- What textbooks and supplementary materials are used?

- What kind of teaching methods are used? (For example, formal teaching, group learning, emphasis on translation.)

- Does the school subscribe to any foreign language magazines or newspapers?

- What opportunities are there for exchange visits?

- Are pupils streamed for language lessons or are languages taught to mixed-ability classes?

The last question may require some explanation. In the past, languages were taught only to the academically more able pupils since it was felt that learning a language was a rather difficult exercise. Now that all secondary school pupils learn languages, there are some schools that stream pupils for language learning while others do not.

Generally speaking, the more homogeneous a class the more effective the learning process, and this applies, many believe, to language learning in particular. Unless mixed-ability classes are organised extremely well, the brighter pupils may get frustrated with the slow progress of the lessons, while those with less aptitude can become discouraged because they feel they are getting left behind.

WHEN SHOULD A CHILD START A LANGUAGE?

There is a body of opinion that feels that the younger a child starts to learn a foreign language the better. This certainly makes sense in bilingual situations, where a child has exposure to two languages in everyday life — in expatriate communities abroad, in Welsh-speaking communities in Wales, for instance.

However, such schemes work less well in other circumstances. Attempts have been made to start language learning, usually French, in state primary schools — often to great acclaim. Unfortunately, in most cases no provision is made for early starters when they move on to the secondary level of education and pupils have to start the language once more from scratch.

In Scotland the situation is more promising. Foreign languages are gradually being introduced into all primary schools and the secondary school system will adjust accordingly. South of the border a few state schools are organising language tuition (often out of school hours) partly in response to parental pressure, but the picture is very patchy.

So, while you may want your child to learn a foreign language from an early age, it is not very practical in organisational terms. There is little point in embarking on learning a language if he will only have to repeat the same process at a later date. Besides, there is evidence to suggest that an 11-year-old can learn a foreign language quicker and more effectively than an 8-year-old.

However, language learning at any age deserves encouragement. If your child shows an interest in languages, you could find a tutor or provide him with language books, videos or audio cassettes, particularly if you are planning a holiday abroad where he will have a chance to use the language in context. Usborne, for instance, publish a number of attractive language books for young beginners and there is *The BBC Language Course for Children* with animated videos and audio-cassettes distributed by Early Advantage. And there are a number of private initiatives such as Le Club Français with branches throughout Britain which teach foreign languages to children of primary school age by means of games and songs.

THE ROLE OF PARENTS

Do parents have a role to play in the language learning of their children or should they be content to leave it to the school? British parents tend to be more 'laid back' in this respect than some of the parents I have met on the Continent who either engage part-time language tutors for their offspring or bundle them off to language classes out of school hours.

While I would be the last to discourage young people from spending extra time on language learning, there is a danger of overdoing it; too many demands put on a child can prove counter-productive. However, if your son or daughter seems to be struggling with the language, by all means have a discreet word with his or her language teacher and take note of any suggestions.

It may so happen that the school is to blame for the lack of progress, for reasons I touched on in the first part of this chapter. Another possibility is that it does not have facilities for teaching the language(s) you would like your child to learn. In such cases, you may well need to take matters into your own hands and explore ways of supplementing your child's learning.

In most cases this will involve expenditure on your part, although local authority colleges may be prepared to waive or reduce fees for anyone in full-time education. The following possibilities are also worth considering:

- *A part-time tutor*
  This could prove an expensive option. Normally people settle for just one or two lessons a week, but if two or three children share a tutor the per capita cost is lower.

- *A course*
  In many places on the Continent language schools offer special courses for young people; a few in the United Kingdom do the same. Investigate also local authority institutions, such as community colleges and adult education colleges as well as foreign and private cultural institutes (in London and some other large cities).

SUPPLEMENTING THE LANGUAGE LEARNING PROCESS

Language learning may seem rather pointless to a young person if there is little opportunity to practise what has been learned. It is therefore important to set learning in some kind of context by establishing links with the countries using the target language and providing essential back-up.

- *A good dictionary or phrase-book*
  This is the essential back-up to which I referred. State schools in Britain supply pupils with basic textbooks which may

Children and Language Learning 77

contain a glossary of words used in the text, but dictionaries are not usually issued. Sooner or later your child will need to look up a word which does not appear in the glossary at the end of the textbook.

- *Foreign language magazines and newspapers*
  There are a number of publications for learners of modern languages from publishers such as Mary Glasgow Publications and Authentik, and it may be possible to order these through the school. As your child becomes more proficient, you could try foreign newspapers, magazines and comics. If your local newsagent does not stock any foreign publications as a matter of course, he can usually obtain them. In London the Soho area is full of newsagents with newspapers from all round the world.

- *A pen-friend*
  This can be a useful way of stimulating interest not only in the foreign language but also in the country and its people. Your child's school may be able to provide you with a contact; otherwise try a local twinning committee (the majority of UK districts and boroughs are twinned with towns in Germany and France) or contact the Belfast office of the Central Bureau. If a number of parents have a similar idea you might even put an advertisement in a foreign newspaper or journal. Many of these are represented in London.

- *Radio and TV language courses*
  The BBC and other broadcasting organisations transmit some very interesting and lively language series which are a useful complement to work that is studied in class. Some courses for children are also available on video cassette.

- *Cassettes, records and radio*
  While not many record shops in Britain stock foreign records and cassettes, you can usually find records of French, Spanish and Italian artistes such as Julio Iglesias and Charles Aznavour in public library record collections. Don't overlook foreign radio transmissions, though in some areas reception is poor and you may need a short-wave set.

- *Films, video and TV*
  Watching foreign films with subtitles is a pleasurable way of learning a language, whether in the cinema or on TV. If you

have a satellite dish you will also be able to pick up foreign language transmissions from other countries.

- *Computer language games*
  If your child is a computer buff and has his or her own machine, you could try hiring or buying a computer program designed to assist language learning. CILT publish a list of distributors of computer software for language learning.

VISITS ABROAD

It is essential to differentiate between visits that are purely for pleasure and those which have a serious linguistic purpose. Sending your children off on a skiing trip with the school in the French Alps will do little, if anything, to improve their French. They will be surrounded by their peers and possibly never get a chance to practise the language. The same is usually true, though perhaps to a lesser extent, of family holidays abroad.

If you wish your child to practise a foreign language he needs to be put in a situation where he is surrounded by speakers of the language and has no option but to speak it. This might take one of the following forms:

- *Twinning trips*
  Some schools or towns have group exchanges with schools or towns on the Continent where young people are offered hospitality by local families and may attend classes in local schools. Usually the groups are accompanied by teachers or other responsible adults.

- *Individual home stays*
  Another idea is to place your child with a family either on an exchange basis or as a paying guest. Personal contacts are always the best, but if you do not know of any families who would offer hospitality, you could contact your local twinning committee, the Central Bureau for Educational Visits and Exchanges or a specialist agency, such as International Links.

- *Summer courses*
  Hundreds of thousands of foreign children flock to Britain for language courses every summer, and there are similar arrangements in other countries for youngsters from this country. Usually pupils spend half the day studying, and the other half

is free. You can either contact a foreign school direct or make arrangements through one of the agencies in this country which offer a study package, such as Euro-Academy Outbound and SIBS.

References: *Study Holidays: An Authoritative Guide to European Language Learning* (Central Bureau for Educational Visits and Exchanges).
Where and How? (Wie und Wo Verlag).

- *Au-pairing*
  This is an option mainly for girls in their late teens and upwards. They live with a family and receive board, accommodation and sometimes a small allowance in return for undertaking light tasks in the household (which often involve looking after children). Full details are available in *The Au Pair and Nanny's Guide* (Vacation Work Publications, Oxford).

- *Other exchange schemes*
  There are a number of initiatives afoot, particularly within the European Community, to promote exchanges of young people in professional, vocational and technical education under the LINGUA Programme (c/o Central Bureau for Educational Visits and Exchanges. Tel: (071) 224 1477).

A longer stay abroad

One idea worth considering is that of sending your child off to another country for a term or even for a whole year, to stay with relations or trusted friends. However, it is important to consider the implications. While it may work well with a 12-year-old, it could hamper the educational progress of a 15-year-old, since this is a time of life when important examinations are looming up.

The same problem afflicts sixth-formers, and, in view of the intense competition for places in higher education, parents have reason to be anxious not to jeopardise their son's or daughter's studies. There are, however, schools in a number of countries which prepare their pupils for the International Baccalaureate, a qualification which is equivalent to 'A' Level and is internationally regarded.

Contact the International Baccalaureate Office, 18 Woburn Square, London WC1H 0NS. Tel: (071) 637 1682 for further details.

A growing number of young people are keen to spend a year in a foreign country between finishing school and starting work, and this could be the ideal time for them to practise their language skills abroad. The book *A Year Off* (CRAC/Hobsons) offers useful advice, as does Nick Vandome's *How to Spend a Year Abroad* (How To Books).

CHILDREN IN SPECIAL SITUATIONS

So far I have concentrated on children in English-speaking environments who do not come into contact with foreign languages outside the classroom. Others find themselves in situations where they are exposed to two or perhaps a variety of languages in their everyday life. When it comes to language learning children like this are at an advantage.

- *A bilingual family background*
  Where the mother tongue of each parent is different, children are in an enviable situation, since they have the opportunity to become bilingual from an early age. I have sometimes been astonished to find a young child conversing fluently with his mother in one language and with his father in another.
  But won't exposure to two languages mean that the child gets muddled up? Not necessarily, unless the parents switch between one language and the other. In due course the child will become more accomplished in one language than in the other, and this will be determined by external factors — such as the language used at school and in the media — rather than family ones.

Reference: *The Bilingual Family Newsletter*, Multilingual Matters Ltd, Bank House, 8A Hill Road, Clevedon, Avon BS21 7HH.

- *Expatriate children*
  Expatriate children are also at an advantage if they are based in a country where a foreign language is spoken, though if they tend to be restricted to their own community (e.g. at an army base) they may not necessarily take advantage of their circumstances. By playing with local children, watching TV and participating in everyday tasks such as shopping, they will assimilate a good deal of the language with little effort.
  Sometimes the language of the country concerned is included on the curriculum of the school that they attend; but if you are

intending to stay in the country for some time you might investigate whether there are any bilingual schools your children could attend. To pack them off to a local school where instruction is in the vernacular might also be possible if they already have some knowledge of the language in question. If not, the experience could prove traumatic and might set back their educational progress.

- *Ethnic minorities*
  Concern is sometimes expressed for children from ethnic minorities because they do not speak English at home. However, it is wrong to categorise them as 'disadvantaged'. In the long run they will doubtless prove to be more adept linguists than their monolingual peers.

So if you are a parent whose mother tongue is not English, there is no real need to make an effort to become an English-speaking household in order to help your children to progress at school. Nurture your mother tongue and encourage your children to have a pride in it. Their lives will be much enriched thereby.

In some education authority areas provision is made for children to learn their mother tongue, but more often than not it is left to individual parents to make their own aarrangements. In the larger cities there may be cultural associations which organise part-time courses or can provide tutors. Alternatively, you could obtain reading materials from bookshops or through public libraries and assist your child yourself.

The National Council for Mother Tongue Teaching, 52 Park Road, Rugby CV21 2QH. Tel: (0788) 544516 should be able to advise. See also under the relevant language entry in Appendix A.

7
Language Training in Organisations

So far I have considered the individual language learner. In this final chapter I turn my attention to language training in organisations.

In much of Western Europe language training is accorded a very high priority. German, French and Italian companies are prepared to invest large sums to ensure their key staff are proficient in two or three foreign languages; some are prepared to send their top executives on intensive residential courses costing up to £2,000 a week. By contrast, Britain and other countries of the English-speaking world seem as if they are still in the 'Dark Ages' as far as learning foreign languages is concerned.

This point is well illustrated by an exercise conducted by the British Institute of Management. The Institute sent business letters written in French, German, Spanish and Italian to 3,000 managers. Of the 584 who replied just 44 per cent could understand the French version, 14 per cent the German, 5 per cent the Spanish and only 4 per cent the Italian. Worse still, only 23 per cent reckoned they could reply in French, 9 per cent in German and 2 per cent in Italian and Spanish.[1]

Lack of linguistic ability at the top is often replicated all down the line. The lower echelons reason that, if the top brass of the company have managed to progress to their present positions with no knowledge of foreign languages, clearly there is little point in bothering about them.

However, change is in the air. In Britain a number of firms with no tradition of language training are beginning to feel uneasy, and with good cause. In the decades since the country acceded to the European Community, Continental firms seem to have been extremely successful at selling into the British market, more so than many British firms on the Continent. Their salesmen come to

---

[1] Pearce, G.: *'Bonjour, Europe'* — *Languages and the British Manager* (British Institute of Management, Management House, Cottingham Road, Corby, Northants NN17 1TT).

Britain with complete mastery of English and sound extremely convincing. British salesmen go to the Continent speaking excellent English, too, but they seem to clinch fewer deals.

Why? Elsewhere in this book I have stated the belief that the language of business is the language of one's customer. Yet still many managers remain sceptical about the worth of foreign language competence in their own firms and do nothing. Others attempt to respond to the challenge of Europe, but their response is half-hearted, either because they are unsure how to set about it or because they are not prepared to invest sufficiently in training. Only an enlightened few are prepared to go the whole way and institute a full-blooded language training programme. In the long run they will reap the benefit.

However, there are pitfalls for the unwary. Let us start with a cautionary tale.

INEFFECTIVE LANGUAGE TRAINING

Dudley Eager of Eager Electronics has decided to mount an export drive to Continental Europe and has been told that the key to success is to have staff who speak foreign languages. Since hardly any of his employees are adept in this area he decides to set aside a few hundred pounds of the training budget for language classes. He engages a teacher of French who has just retired from a local school and announces that there will be French lessons after work every Wednesday open to those who want to improve their language skills.

Some twenty or so people register an interest in learning French, but when Dudley drops in on the class some weeks later he gets a shock. A mere half a dozen of his employees are left on the course, and most of these are unlikely to need to use a foreign language other than on holiday. The others have simply dropped out.

What has gone wrong? Bad teaching? Lack of motivation? Inertia? Or what? Dudley decides to investigate.

He discoves that Miss A, who already has 'O' Level French, left because she found the course too elementary. Mr B, on the other hand, decided after two lessons that language learning was beyond him and gave it up as a bad job. Mrs C, a secretary, decided the course had little relevance to her needs: she wants to learn how to write business letters not discuss holidays and read Molière. Mr D from the export department left the course because he felt he was being upstaged by a subordinate whose French was better than his. Mr E had gone off on a business trip to Toulouse two weeks after the course started, and found it had been of no use at all. High-flier Miss F had never even started the course; she felt that learning French was a waste of time since most of the firm's customers were in Spanish- and German-speaking countries.

Dudley Eager throws up his hands in despair: all his good intentions appear to have come to naught. Thoroughly disillusioned, he decides to cut his losses: he suspends the class and vows never to repeat the experiment.

Yet instead of roaring off in high dudgeon, he would do well to ponder on the experience, investigate where mistakes had been made and make suitable adjustments. Here are a few of the errors he committed:

- He allowed people to select themselves. For training, people need to be selected.

- He assumed that everybody attending the course would have reached the same level in the language. As it turned out, some participants were virtual beginners, while others had a good basic knowledge. It is difficult for even the greatest teacher in the world to maintain interest when levels are so disparate.

- He failed to indicate to the teacher the kind of activities his staff were likely to need a foreign language for.

- He made no allowance for hierarchical differences within the class. Senior staff may feel uncomfortable learning with juniors — and vice versa.

- The language programme he envisaged was inflexible. It could not cope, for instance, with the urgent language training needs of Mr E.

- He may well have selected the wrong language. While French is undoubtedly important, there are many more German-speakers in Europe than French-speakers.

- He may have made a mistake in his choice of teacher. Someone with an industrial or commercial training background would perhaps have been more appropriate.

One might argue that the course was relatively cheap to organise, but was it cost-effective? A general course without carefully defined aims is not likely to achieve much; and paying out money for no tangible results is plainly wasteful.

I am not suggesting that every decision-maker commits the same errors as Mr Eager. But language training happens to be an area where many executives feel completely at sea, and it is worth while trying to get things as right as possible first time round rather than learning by trial and error.

There is a lesson to be learned from Mr Eager's approach. For effective language training within an organisation you have to select the RIGHT people, and teach them the RIGHT language skills for the RIGHT language using the RIGHT methods. In other words, the training has to be properly focused.

PUTTING LANGUAGE TRAINING INTO FOCUS

How do you set about this task? For a start you need to pose the following three questions:

Which staff need to use foreign languages?

Staff involved in export marketing will be the most obvious candidates for language tuition since they may well be making foreign business trips or appearing at exhibitions. Even those who do not venture abroad, such as secretarial and clerical staff, are included, since they may have to deal with enquiries over the phone and with correspondence in foreign languages.

If your contract with a foreign firm includes a training, installation or maintenance component, technical and supervisory staff will also require some type of training; and the same applies to any representative you appoint to an overseas territory. There may also be a need for certain key staff to represent your organisation at conferences in other countries.

It is more than likely that foreign clients will want to visit you, in which case they will need to be entertained and shown around. Technical staff and other members of the management team will probably be involved, but one should not overlook less senior staff who are in the first line of fire, as it were, in dealing with clients, such as the driver who meets clients from the airport. Telephonists also need language training.

These suggestions are by no means unrealistic or excessively idealistic. In order to make an impact on foreign clients right from the outset you need to give the impression that the whole company, not just a few individuals, is trying to meet them on their terms.

What activities do they need languages for?

Once you have identified staff who could benefit from language training, you need to consider in which situations they are likely to use the language. The following list should trigger a few ideas:

Giving presentations and talks

Meeting with clients

Negotiating deals

Manning an exhibition stall

Attending conferences and seminars

Training or supervising non-English-speakers

Surviving on foreign business trips

Welcoming visitors

Socialising with clients

Compiling reports from foreign language sources

Preparing publicity material or manuals in foreign languages

Dealing with people over the phone

Dealing with correspondence

Reading technical manuals and brochures

Checking contracts written in different languages.

Which languages are most important to your organisation?

This is a matter I dealt with at length in Chapter 2. Clearly in a commercial enterprise you will opt for the language(s) of your major customers or of countries for which you have expansion plans.

Language Competence Chart

DEFINITIONS OF LEVELS PLOTTED ON THE PROFILE OF PERFORMANCE

	Speaking/Interactive Skills	Listening and Reading	Writing
LEVEL 5	Takes the initiative in speaking and participates confidently in conversation/exchanges, with generally fluent presentation. Responds with confidence and spontaneity.	Is able to seize the essentials of a spoken/written source with confidence. Can select and interpret information appropriately and understands detail accurately.	Conveys information effectively, in appropriate style and with clarity.
LEVEL 4	Plays an active, and usually fluent, part in conversation/exchanges. Responds well, though sometimes searches for words.	Distinguishes without too great difficulty between essential elements and less important detail in a spoken/written source. May nevertheless make some minor errors of interpretation that do not affect overall understanding.	Conveys most of the required information with clarity, though some inappropriate usage may occasionally intrude.
LEVEL 3	Can maintain a conversation/exchange, though may need occasional repetition and speech will be halting at times. Can follow the spoken word at normal speed sufficiently to grasp the essentials and make a response.	Succeeds in grasping the central message of a spoken/written source, but peripheral detail may intrude. Some less significant detail will be distorted.	Provides a fair amount of comprehensible information and achieves reasonable success in conveying the message, but some errors of structure impede communication.
LEVEL 2	Attempts to participate in conversation/exchanges, but lacks fluency and will need some repetition or paraphrase. Takes time in responding but could cope within a work situation.	Is able to follow the general import of a spoken/written source, but fails to discriminate between central and peripheral information. A number of details will be inaccurate.	Provides most elements of information required. There will be errors of structure, but they are not serious enough to distort the basic message.
LEVEL 1	Does not display any initiative in conversation/exchanges. Fails to make appropriate responses and speech is full of hesitations. Could not function within the work situation.	Fails to grasp either the essentials or significant details of a spoken/written source. Makes many serious errors of comprehension. The message is garbled.	Does not provide important elements of the information required. Meaning only comes through occasionally. Reader has difficulty in understanding.

Reproduced with the kind permission of LCCI

Generally speaking, it is more sensible to opt for a language which features among my 'Top Ten'. However, in the case of individuals whom you are considering sending abroad as representatives or technical experts in certain countries, clearly they need tuition in the main language of that particular country.

Once you have completed this preliminary investigation, you will doubtless find that a fairly complicated picture emerges. You need to concentrate not on one language, but on several, and different people need to use foreign languages for different tasks. Some will need to concentrate on speaking and understanding people; others will need to have predominantly passive skills (i.e. understanding presentations and texts); some will need to achieve a high degree of proficiency (e.g. for negotiations); others will need just a basic knowledge, but perhaps of several languages.

Unless you have sufficient in-house expertise, it makes sense to engage the services of a language training consultant for advice on how to set up a training programme. A good consultant would then assess the language levels of the staff recommended for training and suggest ways of improving their competence. (See chart showing Language Competence Levels on page 87.)

He needs to be made aware from the outset of the constraints you are working under. Among them are the following:

- *Time constraints*
  Some staff may have to learn a language in a short time before an overseas tour.

- *Financial constraints*
  Most training departments have to operate within a fixed budget which is, alas, never sufficient to cover all training needs.

- *Availability of staff*
  Some staff are constantly on the move and it is difficult to tie them down to regular classes. Others are not available for classes during working hours.

- *Facilities*
  While most offices and plants have some kind of premises for training, it may not be suitable or available for language training.

It is quite possible that the consultant will come up not with one, but with a number of solutions. They are likely to be variations on the following schemes:

- Special tailor-made courses either on your own premises or that of the training provider. This would be an excellent solution if there are a number of people in the organisation whose needs are virtually identical. However, it might be beyond the reach of smaller firms unless they decide to pool their resources.

- The provision of self-study materials or open-access learning. This might be the only solution for staff who find difficulty in tying themselves down to a particular schedule.

- Enrolling staff on courses that are already scheduled. Junior employees, for instance, might best be accommodated on a part-time course leading to a recognised qualification at a local college, while others might attend evening courses paid for or subsidised by the organisation.

- A combination of study methods, such as a short intensive course followed up by self-study and/or occasional telephone tutorials.

Two final points. If your organisation is subject to seasonal work fluctuations, it makes sense to schedule your language training programmes for the slack periods. Also, the easy option of holding language classes after work is not always the best one, since by the end of the day people's brains are tired and their thoughts are focused on other matters. Employees are likely to learn more quickly if courses are held earlier in the day when their minds are fresh.

PREPARING STAFF FOR OVERSEAS ASSIGNMENTS

Where staff are being sent abroad for an extended visit it makes sense to give them a fairly intensive language course before they go. If they already have a qualification in the language, one should think in terms of a fortnight at least; but if they are starting from scratch, you are probably talking in terms of months. Public-sector employees are sometimes sent on much longer courses; a former member of the services tells me he underwent four years' full-time training in Chinese.

Company executives may pale at the thought of periods of training of this order; but I have come across a few who felt it worth while to send key staff off for three to six months' intensive language tuition. Unlike their foreign counterparts, British firms hesitate to commit large sums of money to language training, and even if they are prepared to do so, they tend to underestimate the amount of time it takes for a person to learn a language.

Too often decisions on language training are made at the eleventh hour, and a training provider is contacted to see if a course can be arranged a mere week or so before a person is due to leave for an overseas assignment. This is hardly an ideal situation for either the provider or the trainee himself, who is probably so preoccupied with preparations for his departure that he is unable to devote his full attention to instruction.

However, some form of language training is better than no language training at all. There are some useful courses around which provide an introduction to a particular language, such as Arabic Services' one week introductory course in Arabic at the School of Oriental and African studies in London.

Yet one needs to appreciate that the trainee will emerge from a short period of tuition with only limited skills survival language, in other words. He may be able to ask his way around, but he will certainly not be up to making presentations in the target language. To attain that level a much higher amount of language input will be required.

Once he has mastered the rudiments of language at home, it makes good sense for the staff member to undergo language training in the country of his assignment before he actually gets down to work there, provided there are suitable learning facilities. International language training organisations are often in a position to provide a continuation course on arrival if the trainee has done a course with a sister establishment at home.

Apart from understanding the language of the country to which he is posted, an employee also needs to know something about the attitudes and customs of the people among whom he will be working, a point that I stress in *How to Get a Job Abroad*. Organisations such as SOAS and the Centre for International Briefing are in a position to offer both language courses and briefings on different countries; and the Association of Language Export Centres can put you in touch with other organisations providing such a service.

FINDING A TRAINING PROVIDER

Chapter 3 lists different types of language training delivery systems, though not all of these are necessarily in a position to handle industrial training requirements. Inevitably you will need to shop around to find out which organisation can offer the type and range of training you need at a competitive price. You may even find that you have to engage the services of more than one organisation.

I recommend trying local colleges, and universities for a start, since many of them enjoy close links with local industries and organisations and have a mandate to render as much assistance to them as possible. Thanks to the Professional, Industrial and Commercial Updating Programme (PICKUP) of the Department of Education and Science in Britain, local colleges are now able to offer a more flexible service for firms wishing to update the skills of their employees than was once the case.

If your nearest college cannot offer the type of service you require, try your nearest Language Export Centre (see Appendix C), consult the PICKUP Training Directory or contact the nearest Training Access Point of the Training Agency. Private-sector language training organisations also deserve investigation. Many of them are highly professional and reputable organisations geared up to the needs of commercial clients. Some have facilities for residential intensive courses as well as branches abroad.

Whether you call on an organisation or an individual to deal with your language training needs, there are questions you should ask:

- What experience do you have of company language training?

- What methods of teaching do you use?

- What kind of teaching materials (e.g. books) would you use?

- What are your qualifications?

- How long will it take you to teach employees the necessary language skills?

- Have you any clients similar to us who can recommend you?

- What extra costs are there on top of the tuition fees (for course books, audio tapes, equipment, etc.)?

MEASURING RESULTS

Earlier in this chapter I referred to the need to focus training. This process involves setting out specific targets and later on measuring the extent to which the targets have been achieved. It is important not only to monitor the progress of the individual trainee but also the effectiveness of the training organisation.

It is not unreasonable to expect the trainer to write a progress report on each trainee at the end of the course indicating the level he has reached and the type of skills he has acquired, together with recommendations for future training. Training organisations normally have a system of progress tests designed to measure individual improvement, and where such tests are used the training officer should be informed of the results.

There are also a number of public examinations with a strong practical bent for which trainees (particularly the more junior ones) could be entered. In the United Kingdom the examing bodies include the City and Guilds of London Institute, the Royal Society of Arts and Commerce (RSA), the Institute of Linguists with its Examinations in Languages for International Communication, and the London Chamber of Commerce and Industry (LCCI).

The last named is also involved in a new flexible language training initiative — the Foreign Languages at Work Scheme (FLAW) — which provides targets of attainment based on assessment rather than formal examinations. The end-of-course certificate indicates the level of attainment of the individual course member in the various communication skills. Although the scheme was designed with the 16-to-19 age group in mind it is proving suitable for adults as well because of its practical emphasis and the fact that trainees are not expected to pass an examination at the end. Many of the examinations have been revamped to bring their qualifications in line with the national vocational qualifications laid down in the UK by the Languages Lead Body.

However, you do not have to insist on your staff taking an examination, particularly the more mature ones. While examinations are useful tools, the best proof of the effectiveness of a course is how well people cope on a day-to-day basis in foreign language situations.

References: *Foreign Languages at Work* (London Chamber of Commerce and Industry).

Hagen, S. (ed.): *Languages in British Business: An Analysis of Current Needs* (Newcastle upon Tyne Polytechnic Products Ltd/ CILT).

Jones, R.: *How to Get a Job Abroad* (How To Books, Plymbridge House, Estover Road, Plymouth PL6 7PZ).

Operation Speakeasy (Argus Video Productions, 52 Church Street, Melton Constable, Norfolk NR24 2LE). Video showing how a language auditor devises corporate language training policy.

Appendix A
Languages of the World

KEY

Level
Languages are rated according to the level of difficulty. Level 1 languages are fairly easy for an English-speaker to learn, Level 2 languages may take longer, Level 3 languages are the most difficult of all, usually because of their unfamiliar scripts. However, a Level 3 language learned in Roman transcription would approximate more closely to a Level 2 language.

Description
A brief indication of the geographical range of the language, its importance and (in the case of the more widespread languages) potential difficulties for the learner. For a more detailed description of the language please refer to Campbell, G. L.: *Compendium of the World's Languages* (Routledge, 1991).

Reference
This section indicates some of the courses which are readily available, but is by no means complete. Sometimes this is for reasons of space: there is simply not enough room to include every French, German, or Spanish course, for instance. In certain cases where a course is one of a well-known series (e.g. Teach Yourself) I have not always supplied full details of the book. For details of these series as well as publishers and distributors please turn to Appendix B.

Tuition
Selected organisations which either offer courses or can put you in touch with a tutor of that particular language, the addresses of which are listed in Appendix C. In the case of the more commonly taught foreign languages, you are advised to get in touch with colleges and language schools in your locality in the first instance.
Note: CILT, the Centre for Information on Language Teaching and Research, publishes leaflets offering further information on certain languages. *Floodlight* is a brochure giving details of part-time courses in the London area published by the Association of London authorities; SOAS is the School of Oriental and African Studies, London University; SSEES is

Appendix A

the School of Slavonic and East European Studies, London University. Publishers' addresses appear in Appendix B and other addresses in Appendix C.

THE LANGUAGES

Afrikaans Level: 1
A derivative of Dutch and one of the official languages of South Africa spoken by some 3.5 million people.
    Shalkwyk, H.: *Teach Yourself Afrikaans* (Hodder & Stoughton).
    How to Say it in Afrikaans (Department of Immigration, Pretoria, South Africa).
    Other courses: Conversaphone: Language/30; Linguaphone, PILL; Language Learn.

Albanian Level: 2
The national language of Albania with some 4.5 million speakers in Albania and south-eastern former Yugoslavia.
    Zymberi, I.: *Colloquial Albanian* (Routledge).
    Mazi, Z.: *A Guide Book to Albanian — English–Albanian Phrase Book* (Nentori Publishing House, Albania).
    Newmark, L. *et al.*: *Spoken Albanian* (Spoken Language Services).

Amharic Level: 3
The official language of Ethiopia spoken by some 7 million people and belonging to the Semitic group of languages.
    FSI Basic Amharic (Audio-Forum). Course book and 26 cassettes.
    Kebede, M. and Murphy, J.: *Amharic Newspaper Reader* (Dunwoody).
    Spoken Amharic (SLS).
    Tuition: Africa Centre; *Floodlight*; SOAS.

Arabic Level: 3
The national language of 18 Arab countries stretching from Morocco in the west to Oman in the east and the mother tongue of some 180 million people. It is also the language of one of the world's great religions, Islam, and is studied by Muslims all over the world.
    When choosing a course one needs to decide whether to learn Classical Arabic — the language of the Koran — or Modern Colloquial Arabic — the modern spoken variety. There are various dialects of modern Arabic: North African/Maghreb Arabic in Morocco, Algeria, Tunisia and Libya; Egyptian Arabic; Levantine Arabic in Syria, Iraq, Jordan and Palestine; Gulf Arabic in Kuwait, Saudi Arabia, the United Arab Emirates, Oman, Qatar and Yemen. Within these dialects there are various sub-dialects. Generally speaking, Levantine and Egyptian Arabic are understood throughout the whole region. Classical Arabic is understood by educated Arabs.

If you are interested principally in speaking Arabic there are a number of courses with Roman transcription, though not all sounds in Arabic are readily transcribable. If you have the time there is much to be said for attempting to learn the written language in parallel as this will enable you eventually to use dictionaries and read newspapers. Particular problems: script, pronunciation, grammar, vocabulary.

Abboud, P. F. and McCarus, E. N.: *Elementary Standard Arabic* (Cambridge University Press), 2 volumes.

Ali Syed, *Arabic for Beginners* (Hippocrene).

Francis, T. and Frost, M.: *Macmillan Arabic Course* (Macmillan). 2 volumes.

FSI Modern Written Arabic (Audio-Forum). Two volumes with cassettes.

FSI Basic Saudi Arabic Course (Audio-Forum).

Harvey, D.: *Spoken Arabic* (Hodder & Stoughton).

Erwin, W. M.: *A Basic Course in Iraqi Arabic* (Georgetown UP).

Harrell, R. S.: *A Basic Course in Moroccan Arabic* (Georgetown UP).

Mitchell, T. F. and Barker, D.: *Introduction to Arabic* (BBC).

Wightwick, J. and Gaafar, M.: *Mastering Arabic* (Macmillan/Hippocrene). Coursebook and 2 cassettes.

McLoughlin, L.: *Colloquial Arabic — Levantine* (Routledge).

McGuirk, R.: *Colloquial Arabic of Egypt* (Routledge).

Holes, C.: *Colloquial Arabic of the Gulf and Saudi Arabia* (Routledge).

Persson, A., Persson, J. and Hussein, A.: *Sudanese Colloquial Arabic for Beginners* (Summer Institute of Linguistics).

Other courses: Assimil; 'At a Glance' (Barron); Conversaphone; 'Get by in Arabic' (BBC); Linguaphone; 'Now You're Talking' (Barron); SLS; Teach Yourself.

Phrase-books; Berlitz; Hugo; Lonely Planet; Penguin; 'Say it'; Teach Yourself.

Tuition: *Floodlight, Polytechnic of Central London*; Durham University; SOAS (Arabic Services Ltd). *Arabic Language Teaching in the UK* (CLAIMS, Department of Modern Arabic Studies, University of Leeds, Leeds LS2 9JT).

Tuition abroad: American University of Cairo; International Language Institute, Cairo; Yarmouk University Language Centre, Jordan; University of Jordan, Amman, Jordan; Institut Bourguiba, Tunis.

Armenian Level: 3

An ancient Indo-European language with its own script spoken by some 5.5 million people in Armenia and north-western Iran.

Spoken East Armenian. Course book and 6 cassettes (SLS).

Gulian, K. H.: *Elementary Modern Armenian* (Hippocrene).

FSI Basic Armenian (Audio Forum). Course book and 23 cassettes.

Phrase-books: Vocabulearn.

Tuition: SOAS.

Appendix A

Assamese
The language of Assam in north-eastern India is Indo-Aryan.
Learn Assamese through English (Read Well Publications, New Delhi).
Tuition: SOAS.

Basque
The language of the Basque region of northern Spain.
Salturelli, M.: *Basque* (Routledge). A descriptive grammar rather than a course book.
Tuition: *Floodlight*; Euskalduntze Alfabetatze Koordinakundea, Diputazio Kalea 3, 48009 Bilbao, Spain. Tel: (Bilbao) 423 1552.

Bengali Level: 3
The mother tongue of 250 million people in Bangladesh and the Indian Province of East Bengal and immigrant communities in the UK and elsewhere. An Indo-Aryan language.
Hilali, M. R.: *Learning Bengali* (Ruposhi Bangla).
Mukharji, S.: *Teach Yourself Bengali* (Hippocrene).
SOAS Bengali Course (SOAS).
Guha, N. K.: *Learn Bengali through English* (Read Well Publications, New Delhi).
Other courses: Teach Yourself (Hodder and Stoughton).
Tuition: *Floodlight*; Institute of Indian Culture; Ruposhi Bangla.

Breton Level: 1
A Celtic language related to Welsh spoken by some half a million people in the French region of Brittany.
Delaporte, R.: *Beginner's Course in Breton* (Cork University Press).
Morvannou, F.: *Breton sans Peine* (Assimil) Two volumes and 6 cassettes.

Bulgarian Level: 2
The national language of Bulgaria spoken by some 8.5 million people which uses the Cyrillic (Russian) script and is a member of the Slavonic language group.
Ghinima, S. A.: *Bulgarian Textbook for Foreigners* (Nauka, Sofia).
Basic Bulgarian (Audio-Forum).
Hubenova, M. *et al.*: *A Course in Modern Bulgarian* (Collets).
Other course: Conversaphone.
Phrase-book: Alexieva, M. and Paunova, E.: *English-Bulgarian Conversation* (Collets).
Tuition: British–Bulgarian Friendship Society, SSEES.

Burmese Level: 3
The principal language of Burma (Myanmar) with its own cursive script in the Tibeto-Burman language group. (NB: In northern Burma Shan is the more commonly spoken language).

Spoken Burmese (SLS).
Okell, J.: *First Steps in Burmese* (SOAS).
Phrase-books: Lonely Planet.
Tuition: SOAS.

Cambodian (Khmer) Level: 3
The national language of Cambodia spoken by 7 million people in Cambodia, the eastern provinces of Thailand and Cambodian communities around the world, notably in the USA and France. It has an elaborate script written from left to right based on ancient Indian languages, and, while the grammar of the language is fairly straightforward, spelling and pronunciation can cause difficulties. Courses are available in Roman transcription.
Jacob, J. M.: *Introduction to Cambodian* (Oxford University Press)
Huffman, F. E.: *Modern Spoken Cambodian* (Yale University Press).
Huffman, F. E.: *Cambodian System of Writing and Beginning Reader* (Yale University Press).
FSI Khmer (Audio Forum). Two volumes and 48 cassettes. Romanised transcription in Volume I.
Tuition: SOAS; Vietnamese-Lao-Cambodian Community Centre, Whiston Road, London E2.

Catalan Level: 1
A Romance language spoken by 6.2 million people in north-eastern Spain including Barcelona.
Yates, A.: *Teach Yourself Catalan* (Hodder & Stoughton).
Tuition: *Floodlight*.

Chamorro Level: 1
An Austronesian language spoken by 63,000 people on the island of Guam in the Pacific.
Topping, D. M.: *Spoken Chamorro* (University of Hawaii Press).

Chinese Level: 3
There are over 1,000 million Chinese-speakers in China, Taiwan, Hong Kong, Singapore, not to mention communities in South-East Asia, USA, UK, etc. There are six major dialects of Chinese with a common script but not mutually intelligible. The principal dialect, that of Beijing, is known as Mandarin or Putonghua. It is now the national language of the People's Republic of China and Taiwan, and is the language that most courses focus on. However, in Hong Kong and Canton Province, Cantonese is of greater relevance.
There are two major problems for European learners of Chinese:

- *Writing*. Each Chinese word is represented by a character instead of being spelt out using an alphabet. A further complication is that the People's Republic now uses 'simplified' characters while elsewhere the traditional characters are used. A number of courses teach a Romanised version of Chinese, such as 'Pinyin' used in China itself as a teaching aid, and for people who are short of time it makes sense to concentrate on the spoken language rather than try to get to grips with thousands of different characters.

- *Pronunciation*. Apart from having a few unfamiliar consonants Chinese is a tonal language. This means that if the pitch of a particular vowel is modified the meaning of the word is changed. Mandarin/Putonghua has four tones: high level (¯), high rising (´), low rising (˘) and high falling (`). Thus yan = tobacco, yán = salt, yan = to perform, yàn = to swallow.

Teng Su Yu: *Conversational Chinese* (University of Chicago Press).
De Francis, J.: *Beginning Chinese* (Yale University Press).
Fenn, H. C. and Tewksbury, M. G.: *Read Chinese* (Yale University Press). Two volumes and 7 cassettes.
Chinese for Beginners (Foreign Languages Publishing House, Beijing, 1986).
Beijing University: *Modern Chinese — A Basic Course* (Dover).
Pollard, D. E.: *Starting Chinese* (BBC).
Pollard, D. E. and T'ung, P. C.: *Colloquial Chinese* (Routledge).
Swadesh, W.: *Conversational Chinese for Beginners* (Dover).
FSI Basic Cantonese (Audio-Forum). Two volumes and 23 cassettes.
Spoken Taiwanese (SLS).
Spoken Amoy-Hokkien (SLS).
Other courses: 'At a Glance' (Barron); Bilingual; Linguaphone; 'Now You're Talking' (Barron); Teach Yourself (Mandarin and Cantonese); Lancashire C.

Phrase-books: *Chinese Phrase Book for Beginners* (SACU); Berlitz; Lonely Planet; Penguin; 'Say it' (Dover); Vocabulearn.

Tuition: *Floodlight*; University of Westminster; SOAS; Thames Valley University (Ealing).

Chinese Language Courses in the UK (Japanese Language Association).

Tuition Abroad: National University of Singapore; Chinese University of Hong Kong; National Taiwan University (Mandarin Training Centre).

Cornish Level: 1
A now extinct Celtic language once spoken in Cornwall.
Smith, A. S. D.: *Lessons in Spoken Cornish* (Truran Publications).
Grufudd, H.: *Cornish is Fun* (Lolfa).
Tuition: *Floodlight*.

Corsican Level: 1
An Italian dialect spoken on the Mediterranean island of Corsica.
Marchetti, P.: *Le Corse sans Peine* (Assimil).

Creole Level: 1
There are a number of these pidgin or trade languages based on French,

Spanish or Portuguese. A French-based Creole is the mother tongue of some 5 million people on Haiti and elsewhere in the Caribbean, and other French-based versions of Creole are found on the Indian Ocean islands of Réunion and Mauritius. Cap Verde and Guinea-Bissau have a Portuguese-based Creole, while a Spanish-based Creole is spoken in the Dutch Antilles.
    FSI Basic Haitian Creole (Audio-Forum). Course-book and 17 cassettes.
    Telchid, S. and Poullet, H.: *Le Créole sans Peine* (Assimil).
    Howe, C.: *Haitian Creole Reader* (Dunwoody).
    Tuition: *Floodlight*.

Czechoslovak Level: 2
Czech and the related Slavonic language Slovak are spoken by some 15 million people in the Czech and Slovak Republics and neighbouring territories.
    Heim M.: *Contemporary Czech* (Audio-Forum) 3 cassettes plus text.
    Lee, W. R. and Z.: *Teach Yourself Czech* (Hodder & Stoughton).
    Naughton, J.: *Colloquial Czech* (Routledge).
    Sara, M. et al.: *Czech for English-Speaking Students* (Collets).
    Other courses: Conversaphone; Linguaphone.
    Phrase-books: Kollmannova, L.: *Czech-English Conversation* (Collets); Harrap; Language 30; 'Say it' (Dover); *Traveller's Czech* (Collets).
    Tuition: *Floodlight*; SSEES.

Danish Level: 1
There are 5 million speakers of this Germanic language in Denmark, Greenland and the Faroe islands.
    Salling, A.: *Learn to Speak Danish*. Course book and cassettes.
    Koefod, H. A.: *Teach Yourself Danish* (Hodder & Stoughton).
    Spoken Danish (SLS).
    Other courses: Language 30; Linguaphone; Univerb;
    Phrase-books: 'Say it' (Dover).
    Tuition: Danish Cultural Centre; *Floodlight*.

Dutch (Flemish) Level: 1
There are some 13 million speakers in the Netherlands and the northern half of Belgium. It is also spoken in the Netherlands Antilles and Surinam.
    Kuiken, F. and Kalsbak, A.: *Code Nederlands* (Meulenhoff Educatief/ European SB).
    Renier, F. G.: *Colloquial Dutch* (Routledge).
    Shetter, W.: *Introduction to Dutch* (Marinus Nijhoff/Thornes).
    Shoenmakers, A.: *Dutch for Beginners* (Stanley Thornes).
    Trim, J. L. M. et al.: *Levend Nederlands* (Cambridge University Press).
    Koolhoven, H.: *Teach Yourself Dutch* (Hodder & Stoughton).
    Spoken Dutch (SLS).

Other courses: Assimil; Hugo; Language 30; Linguaphone; No-Time; Univerb.

Phrase-books: Berlitz; Hugo; Penguin; 'Say it' (Dover).

Tuition: *Floodlight*. A correspondence course is available from De Lidse Onderwijsintellingen, Postbus 4200, 2350 CA Leiderdorp, Netherlands.

Esperanto Level: 0

An artificial language invented by Zamenhoff in 1887 which has a substantial number of adherents in all parts of the world. Much easier to learn than other languages, and could serve as a useful initiation into language study. The British Esperanto Association offers a free 12-hour introduction to the language.

Downes, W. J.: *Esperanto — A Complete Textbook* (British Esperanto Association, 140 Holland Park Avenue, London W11 4UF. Tel: (071) 727 7821.

Thierry, J.: *L'Espéranto sans Peine* (Assimil).

Cresswell, J. and Hartley, J.: *Teach Yourself Esperanto* (Hodder & Stoughton).

Tuition: *Esperanto Association of Great Britain*.

Estonian Level: 2

A language from the Finno-Ugric language group spoken by 1 million people and the official language of Estonia.

Alexander, T.: *Standard Estonian Grammar* (Acta Universitatis Upsaliensis).

Tauli, V. and Oinas, F. J.: *Basic Course in Estonian* (Mouton, The Hague).

Tuition: SSEES.

Finnish Level: 2

One of the Finno-Ugric group of languages which includes Estonian, Lappish and Hungarian. It is spoken by some 5 million people in Finland.

Aaltio, M. H.: *Finnish for Foreigners* (Otava Press, Helsinki). Two volumes plus cassettes.

Whitney, A. H.: *Teach Yourself Finnish* (Hodder & Stoughton)

Spoken Finnish (SLS).

Other courses: Linguaphone; Univerb.

Phrase-books: 'Say it' (Dover).

French Level: 1

The national language of France and the official or co-official language of 21 countries. It is the mother tongue of some 6 million Canadians (mainly in Quebec Province), and the language of southern Belgium and western Switzerland. It is also spoken widely in Haiti and other islands in the Caribbean, several countries of West and Central Africa, Mauritius and the Malagasy Republic (Madagascar).

The importance of French as the international language *par excellence* has been eclipsed by English in this century. Nevertheless it remains an important lingua franca in Italy, on the Iberian peninsula, in North Africa, certain parts of the Middle East, Cambodia, Laos and Vietnam. It remains the most popular foreign language in British schools and universities. Opportunities to learn French exist everywhere, and there is a wide range of courses and learning materials available. Just a few of these are listed below.

Aries, A. and Debney, D.: *Façon de Parler — Rapid French for Beginners* (Hodder & Stoughton).

Baer, E. and Weber, C.: *French for Starters* (Cambridge University Press).

Beeching, K.: *Basic French* (Longman).

Capelle, G. and Gidon, N.: *Espaces* (Hachette/European SB).

Gruneberg, A. and Lacroix, J.: *Voie Express* (CLE/European SB). Revision course with cassettes.

Harris, J. and Lévêque, A.: *Basic Conversational French* (Holt, Rinehart & Winston).

Mitchell, M.: *Working with French* (Stanley Thornes).

Monnerie, A.: Bienvenue en France (Didier/Hatier/European SB). Video and audio cassettes available.

Neather, E. J.: *Mastering French* (Macmillan).

Bower, M. and Barbarin, L.: *French for Business* (Hodder & Stoughton).

Ducassé, M.: *French for Business* (Limitcode).

Gladkow, J. and Sanders, C.: *Franc Exchange* (Pitman). Open/distance learning package.

Heppel, K., Roberts, N. and Rose, E.: *Marché Conclu: Practical Business French* (Hodder & Stoughton).

Tomlinson, P. and Hartop, G.: *Le Français de Affaires* (Managed Learning).

Other courses: Assimil; 'At a Glance' (Barron); Bilingual; Conversaphone; 'Get by in' (BBC); Linguaphone; 'Listen and Learn' (Dover); 'Now You're Talking' (Barron); PILL; 'Quick and Easy' (Langenscheidt/ Hodder); SLS; Stillitron; Talking Business (Barron); Teach Yourself (French, Business French); Univerb.

Phrase-books: Berlitz; Harrap; High Pines, Hugo; Longman; Penguin; 'Say it' (Dover); Travelmate (Drew); Vocabulearn.

Fula (Fulani)
A language spoken in northern Nigeria and neighbouring countries. Niger-Congo group.
FSI Basic Course (Audio Forum).
Tuition: SOAS.

Gaelic Level: 1
Two versions exist. Scots and Irish Gaelic (for Irish Gaelic please look under 'Irish'). Scots Gaelic is spoken by some 100,000 people in the

north-west of Scotland.
Blacklaw, B.: *Scottish Gaelic — A Progressive Course* (Glasgow University Celtic Department).
Macdonald, J. A.: *Gaidhlig Bheo — Basic Gaelic* (National Extension College). Correspondence course with tapes.
Mackinnon, R.: *Teach Yourself Gaelic* (Hodder & Stoughton).
Maclaren: *Gaelic Self-Taught* (Gairm Publications).
Macleod, J.: *Can Seo — Gaelic course for beginners* (BBC).
Patterson, J. M.: *Gaelic Made Easy* (Gairm Publications).
Thompson, D. S.: *Gaelic Learners' Handbook* (Gairm Publications).
Phrase-book: MacNeill, M.: *Everyday Gaelic* (Gairm Publications).
Tuition: *Floodlight*; Comann Luchd Ionnnsachaidh.

German Level: 1
There are over 100 million native speakers of German in Germany, Austria and Switzerland. It is also very much a lingua franca in Eastern and South-East Europe — particularly former Yugoslavia, Greece, Bulgaria and Turkey — since many nationals of these countries have worked as *Gastarbeiter* in Germany.

Germany is important as a language of science and technology, and because of the economic strength of Germany's economy in particular it is an important language of business (particularly for exporters).

German is more closely related to English than French, and its spelling and pronunciation are fairly logical.

Baltzer, R. A. and Strauss, D.: *Alles Gute* (Langenscheidt). Course with video and audio cassettes.
Doring, P. F.: *Colloquial German* (Routledge).
Eggington, E., Lupson, P. and Embleton, D.: *Working with German* (Stanley Thornes).
Peck, A. J.: *Mastering German* (Macmillan).
Göricke-Driver, G.: *German for Business* (Limitcode).
Griesbach, H.: *Deutsch mit Erfolg* (Langenscheidt).
Paxton, N. and Whelan, A. R.: *German for Business* (Hodder & Stoughton).
Herde, D. and Royce, D.: *Vertrag in der Tasche — Practical Business German* (Hodder & Stoughton).
Howarth, M. and Woodhall, M.: *Making your Mark* (Pitman). Training package.
Taylor, R.: *Deutsch Geschäftlich* (Managed Learning).
Other courses: Accelerated Learning; Amway; 'At a Glance' (Barron); Bilingual; Conversaphone; 'Get by in' (BBC); Linguaphone; 'Listen and Learn' (Dover); 'Now You're Talking' (Barron); 'Quick and Easy' (Langenscheidt/Hodder); PILL; SLS; Stillitron; Talking Business (Barron); Teach Yourself; Univerb.
Phrase-books: Berlitz; Harrap; High Pines; Hugo; 'Say it' (Dover); Travelmate (Drew).
Tuition: Anglo-Austrian Society; Goethe Institut; *Floodlight*.

Glosa
This artificial language is a modified version of Interglossa, a language invented by Professor Lancelot Hogben, and is based on Greek and Latin roots.
Ashby, W. and Clark, R.: *18 Steps to fluency in Euro-Glosa*.
Ashby, W. and Clark, R.: *Glosa Study Pack*.
These and other works on Glosa are available from the Glosa Education Organisation, PO Box 18, Richmond, Surrey TW9 2AU; Tel: (081) 948 8417.

Grebo
One of the Kwa sub-group of African languages (which includes Ibo, Yoruba and Akan) spoken in Liberia.
Innes, G.: *An Introduction to Grebo* (SOAS).
Tuition: SOAS.

Greek Level: 2
There are 10 million speakers of Greek throughout the world in Greece and Cyprus, parts of Albania, former Yugoslavia, Bulgaria and Turkey, as well as in Greek communities in the Middle East, USA, UK and Australia. Much of the interest in Modern Greek springs from the country's importance as a tourist destination, but many people are interested in studying earlier forms of the language in order to study classical or biblical texts. You therefore need to be clear in your mind what kind of Greek you wish to study: Modern Greek, Ancient Greek or Biblical Greek. The Teach Yourself series has books on all three languages.
FSI Greek Basic Course. Three volumes with 30 cassettes.
Papaloizos, T. C.: *Modern Greek* (Papaloizos Publications/Zeno).
Farmakides, A.: *A Manual of Modern Greek* (Yale Univesity Press).
Gambarotta, E. and Stamp, J.: *Breakthrough Greek* (Macmillan).
Harris, K.: *Colloquial Greek* (Routledge).
Kinchin Smith, F. and Malluish, T.: *Teach Yourself Greek* (Hodder & Stoughton)).
Sofroniou, S. A.: *Teach Yourself Modern Greek* (Hodder & Stoughton).
Toffallis, K.: *A Textbook of Modern Greek* (Greek Institute).
Betts, A. and Henry, A.: *Teach Yourself Ancient Greek* (Hodder & Stoughton).
Hudson, D. F.: *Teach Yourself New Testament Greek* (Hodder & Stoughton).
Other courses: Conversaphone; Linguaphone; Listen and Learn (Dover); Univerb.
Phrase-books: Berlitz; Longman; Pan; Penguin; 'Say it' (Dover); 'Quick and Easy', (Langenscheidt/Hodder).
Tuition; *Floodlight*; Greek Institute.

Gujarati Level: 3
Spoken by some 33 million people in the Bombay area of India, this is an Indo-Iranian language which uses a derivative of the Devangari script.

Appendix A

Mavi, B. S.: *Teach Yourself Gujarati* (Mavi Publications) Course book with cassettes.
First Steps in Gujarati (Language Information Centre).
Lambert, H. M.: *Gujarati Language Course* (Cambridge University Press/ Sonex, 381 Whitton Avenue E., Greenford, Middx UB6 0UU).
Tuition: *Floodlight*; Institute of Indian Culture, Bradford and Ilkley Community College.

Hausa Level: 2
A Semitic language spoken by 22 million people in northern Nigeria and neighbouring territories.
FSI Hausa Basic Course (Audio-Forum). Coursebook and 15 cassettes.
Skinner, N.: *Hausa for Beginners* (Skinner, distrib. McGraw Hill).
Kraft, C. H. and Kirk-Greene, A. H. M.: *Teach Yourself Hausa* (Hodder & Stoughton).
Spoken Hausa (SLS).
Tuition: Africa Centre; *Floodlight*.

Hawaiian Level: 2
A Polynesian language which is no longer widely spoken.
Elbert, S.H.: *Spoken Hawaiian* (University of Hawaii Press)
Kahananui, D. M. and Anthony, A. P.: *Let's Speak Hawaiian* (University of Hawaii Press).
Phrase-book: *Hawaiian Phrase Book* (Charles E. Tuttle).

Hebrew Level: 3
A Semitic language spoken by some 3 million people in Israel and Jewish communities around the world. There are two types of Hebrew. Biblical Hebrew will be of interest to scholars and theologians, while tourists and business people will need to apply themselves to Modern Hebrew.
FSI Hebrew Basic Course (Audio-Forum). Course book and 24 cassettes.
Learn and Speak Hebrew (Prolog Publishing/Kuperard). Audio-video course.
Shalom from Jerusalem (Rolnik/Kuperard). Four-part home study course with 40 cassettes.
Achiasaf, O.: *Hebrew for English Speakers* (Kuperard).
Gilnert, L.: *Cik-Chak — A Gateway to Modern Hebrew Grammar* (SOAS).
Hunter, A. V.: *Biblical Hebrew — An Inductive Study for Beginners* (University of America Press).
Kittel, B.: *Biblical Hebrew* (Yale University Press).
Stern, A. and Reif, J. (eds): *Everyday Hebrew* (Kuperard).
Harrison, R. K.: *Teach Yourself Biblical Hebrew* (Hodder & Stoughton).
Tirkel, E.: *Hebrew At Your Ease* (Kuperard). Four tapes and book.
Ziv, E. *et al.*: *Everyday Hebrew for Tourists* (Everyman University, 16 Klausner Street, Ramat Aviv, Tel Aviv 61392 Israel).

Other courses: Bilingual; Language 30; Linguaphone; Listen and Learn (Dover).

Tuition: *Floodlight*: Institute of Jewish Education; Zionist Federation Educational Trust.

Hindi Level: 3
An Indo-Aryan language, it is the co-official language of India (with English) and is spoken principally by 175 million people in northern India (notably Uttar Pradesh, Madhya Pradesh, Bihar, Punjab and Himachal Pradesh). Sometimes known as Hindustani, it is closely related to Urdu, though its volcabulary is influenced by Sanskrit and its script is the Devangari system of writing used for Sanskrit.

Mavi, B. S.: *Teach Yourself Hindustani* (Mavi Publications). Course book and cassette.

Nagra, J. S.: *Hindi Made Easy for Beginners* (Nagra & Nagra).

Rao, M.: *Teach Yourself Hindi* (Hippocrene).

Russell, R.: *A New Course in Urdu and Spoken Hindi for Learners in Britain* (SOAS).

Snell, R. and Weightman, S.: *Teach Yourself Hindi* (Hodder & Stoughton).

Weightman, S. C. R.: *An Introduction to Hindi for the VSO* (SOAS).

Verma, M. K.: *Colloquial Hindi-Urdu* (University of York Department of Languages).

Spoken Hindustani (SLS).

Learn Hindi through English (Read Well Publications, New Delhi).

Kapadia, R. and Zorc, D.: *Hindi Newspaper Reader* (Dunwoody).

Other courses: Conversaphone; Language 30; Linguaphone; 'Get by in' (BBC).

Phrase-books: Lonely Planet; 'Say it' (Dover).

Tuition: *Floodlight*; Indian Cultural Centre, Bradford and Ilkley Community College, *Hindi Urdu Guide* (BBC Education).

Hungarian Level: 2
There are an estimated 14 million speakers of Hungarian in Hungary itself and also in Romania, the Czech and Slovak Republics, and the former USSR. It is one of the Finno-Ugric group of languages and therefore quite unlike most other languages of Europe.

Koski, A. and Mihalyfy, I.: *FSI Basic Hungarian* (Audio-Forum). Two volumes with 38 cassettes.

Banhidi, Z.: Learn Hungarian (Kultura Budapest/Collets).

Koski, A. A. and Mihalyfy, I.: *Basic Course in Hungarian* (Hippocrene).

Kassai, G. and Szende, T.: *Le Hongrois sans Peine* (Assimil).

Payne, J.: *Colloquial Hungarian* (Routledge).

Spoken Hungarian (SLS).

Other courses: Conversaphone; Lancashire C.

Phrase-books: Andra, L. and Murvai, M.: *How to Say it in Hungarian* (Collets); Berlitz; Harrap; Language/30; 'Say it' (Dover).

Tuition: British-Hungarian Friendship Society; *Floodlight*.

Ibo
A Kwa language spoken in eastern Nigeria.
   Igwe, G. E. and Green, M. M.: *Ibo Language Course* (Oxford University Press, Ibadan).
   Tuition: SOAS.

Icelandic Level: 1
A Germanic language which is the national language of Iceland.
   Icelandic Conversation (Audio-Forum). 5 cassettes plus text.
   Glendening, P. J. T.: *Teach Yourself Icelandic* (Hodder & Stoughton).
   Other courses: Linguaphone.

Indonesian Level: 1
An Austronesian language spoken as a first or second language by some 100 million people throughout Indonesia closely related to Malay, from which it differs mainly in vocabulary.
   Liaw, Y. F.: *Standard Indonesian Made Simple* (Times Editions, Singapore).
   Liaw, Y. F.: *Guide to Speaking Indonesian* (Times Editions, Singapore).
   FSI Survival Indonesian (Audio-Forum). Mini-course with 3 cassettes.
   Spoken Indonesian (SLS).
   Kwee, J. B.: *Teach Yourself Indonesian* (Hodder & Stoughton).
   Other courses: Conversaphone; Linguaphone.
   Phrase-books: Lonely Planet; 'Say it' (Dover).
   Tuition: *Floodlight*, SOAS.

Irish (Irish Gaelic) Level: 2
A language related to Scots Gaelic spoken by some 100,000 people in the western parts of the Irish Republic and taught in Irish schools.
   Dillon, M. and O'Croinin, D.: *Teach Yourself Irish* (Hodder & Stoughton).
   O'Siadhail, M.: *Learning Irish — An Introductory Self Tutor* (Yale University Press).
   Wilkes, A.: *Irish for Beginners* (Usborne).
   Other courses: Conversaphone; Linguaphone.
   Phrase-books: O'Donnchadha, D.: *Irish Phrase Book* (Mercier, Eire); *Pocket Irish Phrase Book* (Appletree Press).
   Tuition: *Floodlight*; Foras Na Gaeilge, 26 Cearnóg Mhuirfean, Dublin 2. Tel: Dublin 767283.

Italian Level: 2
The mother tongue of 65 million people in Italy (including Sicily and Sardinia), Corsica, Switzerland and former Yugoslavia. There are also substantial Italian communities in the USA, Argentina and Brazil. Many people are attracted to learning Italian for cultural reasons. It is an easy language to learn, particularly for anyone who is already familiar with French, Latin or Spanish.

Andreis, F.: *Colloquial Italian* (Routledge).
Carsaniga, G.: *Italiano Expresso* (Cambridge University Press).
Carsaniga, G.: *Breakthrough Italian* (Macmillan).
Jackson, J., Wicksteed, K. and Israel, J.: *Ciao* (Nelson).
Messora, N.: *Mastering Italian* (Macmillan).
Sedunary, M. and Guarnuccio, E.: *Sempre Avanti* (CIS Educational/Accent).
Vellacio, L. and Elston, M.: *Teach Yourself Italian* (Hodder & Stoughton).
Spoken Italian (SLS).
Edwards, V. and Shepheard, G.: *Missione Italia — Practical Business Italian* (Hodder & Stoughton).

Other courses: Assimil; At à Glance (Barron); Bilingual; Conversaphone; Hugo; Language 30; Linguaphone; 'Listen and Learn' (Dover); No-Time; 'Now You're Talking' (Barron); PILL; 'Quick and Easy' (Langenscheidt/Hodder); Stillitron; Talking Business (Barron).

Phrase-books: Berlitz; High Pines; Pan; 'Say it' (Dover); Univerb; Vocabulearn.

Tuition: Dante Aligheri Society; *Floodlight*; Italian Institute.

Japanese Level: 3

There are 120 million Japanese speakers mainly in Japan, but there are also Japanese communities in Taiwan, Brazil and the USA (notably Hawaii). The language is distantly related to Korean.

The written language is a combination of Chinese ideographs (kanji) and syllabic characters (hirigana and katagana — each set consisting of 50 letters). Japanese children learn the syllabic characters first of all and then proceed to the ideographs. Fortunately, there are a number of courses teaching spoken Japanese which rely on Roman transcription.

AJALT — Association for Japanese Language Teaching: *Japanese for Busy People* (Kodansha International, 17–14 Otowa 1-chome, Bunkyo-ku, Tokyo 112).

Clarke, H. B. D.: *Colloquial Japanese* (Routledge).
Guest, H.: *Mastering Japanese* (Macmillan–Hippocrene).
Harz Jordan, E. and Noda, M.: *Japanese — The Spoken Language* (Yale University Press). Three volumes.
Inamoto, N.: *Colloquial Japanese* (Charles E. Tuttle).
Martin, S. E.: *Essential Japanese* (Charles E. Tuttle).
Sato, E. M. T. *et al.*: *Japanese Now* (University of Hawaii). Four volumes with tapes.
Schwarz, E. A. and Azawa, R.: *Everyday Japanese* (Harrap).
Takamizawa, H.: *Business Japanese* (Gloview Co. Ltd).
Williams, L.: *Active Japanese* (Longman Paul, New Zealand).
Yoshida, Y.: *Japanese for Beginners* (Gakken Co. Ltd, 4-40-5 Kamikeda, Ohta-ku, Tokyo 145).
Young, J. and Nakajima-Okano, K.: *Learn Japanese* (University of Hawaii). Four volumes. Tapes available direct from University of Hawaii.

Doing Business with the Japanese (Hodder & Stoughton).

Other courses: 'At a Glance' (Barron); Bilingual: 'Get by in' (BBC); Hugo; Linguaphone; 'Listen and Learn' (Dover); 'Now You're Talking' (Barron); 'Quick and Easy' (Langenscheidt/Hodder); SLS; Talking Business (Barron); Teach Yourself; Lancashire C.

Phrase-books: Berlitz; Conversaphone; Hugo; *Japanese Word-and-Phrase Book for Tourists* (Tuttle); Lonely Planet; Pan; 'Say it' (Dover); Vocabulearn.

Tuition: Euro-Japanese Exchange Foundation; *Floodlight*; The Japan Centre; Japan Business Consultancy; Japan Language Association; Sheffield University; SOAS.

Japanese Courses in the UK (Japanese Language Association).

Kannada Level: 3
A Dravidian language spoken by some 25 million people in the Indian state of Karnataka.

Halemane, L. and Leelvathi, M. N.: *An Intensive Course in Kannada* (Central Institute of Indian Languages, Mysore).

Learn Kannada through English (Read Well Publications, New Delhi).

Tuition: SOAS; Institute of Indian Culture.

Korean Level: 3
The national language of the Korean peninsula spoken by some 55 million people. It is believed to be distantly related to Turkish. It has its own syllabic system of writing, but Chinese loan-words are sometimes written in Chinese forms.

FSI Korean (Audio-Forum). Two volumes with 34 cassettes.

Martin, S. E. and Lee, Y.-S. C.: *Beginning Korean* (Charles E. Tuttle).

Martin, S. E.: *Korean in a Hurry* (Charles E. Tuttle).

Spoken Korean (SLS).

Other courses: 'At a Glance' (Barron); Conversaphone; Linguaphone; Talking Business (Barron).

Phrase-books: Berlitz; Lonely Planet; Vocabulearn.

Tuition: SOAS; Westminster College.

Kurdish Level: 3
An Indo-European language related to Persian spoken by an ethnic group living in Turkey, Syria, Iraq, Iran and the south of the CIS.

Tuition: *Floodlight*; SOAS.

Lao Level: 3
The national language of Laos related to Thai and also spoken in northern Thailand.

Hoshino, T. and Marcus, R.: *Lao for Beginners* (Charles E. Tuttle).

Yates, W. and Sayasithsena, S.: *FSI Lao Basic Course* (Audio-Forum).

Tuition: SOAS.

Latin Level: 1
Latin may be a dead language but it is still the lingua franca of the Roman Catholic Church and a must for anyone interested in European history since most documents were written in Latin until just a few centuries ago. Most Western European languages are either derived from or have been influenced by Latin, and it continues to be widely taught.
Basic Latin (National Extension College).
Hendricks: *Latin Made Simple* (Heinemann).
Betts, G. G.: *Teach Yourself Latin* (Hodder & Stoughton).
Tuition: *Floodlight*; Madingley Hall, Cambridge CB3 8AQ; Joint Association of Classical Teachers, 31–34 Gordon Square, London WC1 0PY.

Latvian (Lettish) Level: 2
A Baltic Indo-European language related to Lithuanian and spoken by around 1.4 million people in Latvia.
Easy Way to Latvian (Audio-Forum). 12 cassettes plus text.
Fennell, T. G. and Gelsen, H.: *A Grammar of Modern Latvian* (Mouton, The Hague).
Lazdina, T. B.: *Teach Yourself Latvian* (Hodder & Stoughton). Out of print.
Easy Way to Latvian (Audio-Forum).
Tuition: SSEES.

Letzeburgisch (Luxembourgish) Level: 1
A dialect of German spoken in Luxembourg.
Tuition: Institut pro linguis, Place de l'Eglise 19, 6719 Thiaumont, Belgium. Tel: Arlon 220462.

Lithuanian Level: 1
Spoken by some 3.5 million people in Lithuania, Byelorussia, Poland and the United States, this Baltic language is related to Latvian.
Dambriunas, L. *et al.*: *Introduction to Modern Lithuanian* (Franciscan Fathers, 361 Highland Blvd, Brooklyn, NY 11207).
Other course: Conversaphone.
Tuition: SSEES.

Malay Level: 1
An Austronesian language spoken by 11 million people in Malaysia, Singapore and neighbouring territories. Very closely related to Indonesian.
Parry, J. and Suleiman, S.: *Malay in Three Weeks* (Times Editions, Singapore).
Hamilton, A. W.: *Malay Made Easy* (Times Editions, Singapore).
King, E. S.: *Speak Malay* (Times Editions, Singapore).
Spoken Malay (SLS).
Other courses: Conversaphone; Linguaphone; Teach Yourself.
Tuition: SOAS.

Appendix A

Malayalam Level: 3
A Dravidian language related to Tamil spoken by some 25 million people in the Indian state of Kerala.
Learn Malayalam through English (Read Well Publications, New Delhi).
Tuition: SOAS.

Maltese Level: 2
A form of Arabic using the Roman script and influenced by Italian spoken by 300,000 people on the island of Malta.
Aquilina, J.: *Teach Yourself Maltese* (Hodder & Stoughton).

Maori Level: 1
An Austronesian language spoken by some 100,000 Maoris in New Zealand.
Biggs, B.: *Let's Learn Maori* (A. H. Reed, PO Box 14–029, Wellington 3, New Zealand).
Tuition: SOAS.

Marathi Level: 3
The official language of Maharashtra Province in India spoken by some 52 million people and using the Devanagari script.
Deshpande, R. S. and Salpekar, G. E.: *Teach Yourself Marathi* (Hippocrene).
Chitnis, V.: *An Intensive Course in Marathi* (Central Institute of Indian Languages, Mysore).
Learn Marathi through English (Read Well Publications, New Delhi).
Tuition: SOAS.

Mende Level: 2
One of the languages of Sierra Leone in the Mande sub-group.
Innes, G.: *A Practical Introduction to Mende* (SOAS).
Tuition: SOAS.

Nepali (Pahari) Level: 3
The official language of Nepal spoken by some 9.5 million people in Nepal and neighbouring territories. It is Indo-Aryan and closely related to Panjabi and uses the Devanagari (Sanskrit) alphabet.
Matthews: *Course in Nepali* (SOAS).
Sreshtha, P.: *Nepali — A Conversational Approach* (LCL).
Jarmul, C. and Murphy, J.: *Nepali Newspaper Reader* (Dunwoody).
Phrase-book: Lonely Planet.
Tuition: SOAS.

Norwegian Level: 1
The language of 4 million Norwegians which is intelligible to speakers both of Danish and Swedish.
Berit, A. and Strandskogen, R. *Norsk for Utlendinger.*

Haugen, E. and Chapman, K.: *Spoken Norwegian* (Holt, Rinehart & Winston).
Klouman, S.: *Learn Norwegian* (Aschehoug).
Marm, I. and Sommerfelt, A.: *Teach Yourself Norwegian* (Hodder & Stoughton).
Spoken Norwegian (SLS).
Other courses: Bilingual; Language 30; Linguaphone; Univerb; Lancashire C.
Phrase-books: Berlitz; 'Say it' (Dover); Pan.
Tuition: *Floodlight*.

Oriya Level: 3
The Indo-Aryan language of the Indian state of Orissa spoken by some 25 million and closely related to Bengali.
Learn Oriya through English (Read Well Publications, New Delhi).
Tuition: SOAS.

Persian Level: 3
There are a number of varieties of Persian. Farsi, the official language of Iran, is spoken by 18 million people in Iran and Afghanistan, while Pashto is the official language of Afghanistan spoken by 15 million people living in Afghanistan and Pakistan. Other related languages are Kurdish and Baluchi. The Arabic script is used, but the language is Indo-European.
Marashi, M.: *Contemporary Spoken Persian*. Coursebook and 8 cassettes.
Mace, J.: *Teach Yourself Modern Persian* (Hodder & Stoughton).
Moshiri, L.: *Colloquial Persian* (Routledge).
Spoken Persian (SLS).
Haidari, A. A.: *Modern Persian Reader* (SOAS).
MRM Inc.: *Pashto Newspaper Reader* (Dunwoody).
Other courses: Conversaphone; Linguaphone; Language 30; No-time.
Tuition: *Floodlight*; SOAS.

Pidgin Level: 1
A language with a restricted vocabulary which has grown out of English and used as a lingua franca in Papua New Guinea, the Solomon Islands and the New Hebrides.
Melanesian Pidgin Phrase Book (Lonely Planet).

Pilipino Level: 1
The official language of the Philippines and the first or second language of 50 million Filipinos. It is based on Tagalog, the mother tongue of 11.5 million people of Manila and the surrounding region. An Austronesian language.
Bowen, J. D.: *Beginning Tagalog*. Course book and 24 cassettes.
Ramos, T.: *Conversational Tagalog — A Functional-Situational Approach* (University of Hawaii Press).

Aspillera, P. S.: *Basic Tagalog for Foreigners* (Charles E. Tuttle).
Spoken Tagalog (SLS).
Sarra, A. and Zorc R. D.: *Tagalog Newspaper Reader* (Dunwoody).
Other courses: Conversaphone; No-Time; Language 30.
Phrase-book: Lonely Planet.
Tuition: SOAS.

Polish Level: 2
A Slavonic language spoken by some 40 million people in Poland, the Czech and Slovak Republics, and Russia.

Bisko, W., Karolak, S., Wasilewska, D. and Krynski, S.: *Conversational Polish*. Course book and 8 cassettes.

Bisko, W. et al.: *Beginner's Course of Polish* (Collets).

Corbridge-Patkaniowska, M.: *Teach Yourself Polish* (Hodder & Stoughton).

Mazur, B. W.: *Colloquial Polish* (Routledge).

Rudska, B. and Goczolowa, Z.: *Polish for Foreign Students* (Catholic University of Lublin, Al. Raclawickie 14, 20–950 Lublin, Poland). Two volumes.

Schenker: *Beginning Polish* (Yale University Press). Two volumes.

Stone, G.: *An Introduction to Polish* (Collets).

Swan, O.: *First Year Polish* (Collets).

Other courses: Conversaphone; Language 30; Linguaphone; SLS.

Phrase-books: Berlitz; Harrap; 'Say it' (Dover).

Tuition: *Floodlight*; Polish Cultural Centre; SSEES.

Portuguese Level: 1
There are 120 million speakers of this Romance language, of whom 110 million live in Brazil. The Brazilian form of the language differs in certain respects from the European variety. Portuguese is also spoken to some extent in Macao, Mozambique, Angola, Guinea-Bussau and Goa. It currently stands in eighth place in the league of world languages.

Alvelos Naar, M. E.: *Colloquial Portuguese* (Routledge).

Cook, M.: *Teach Yourself Portuguese* (Hodder & Stoughton).

Graziani, L. B.: *Encontro com o Portugues — A course in Brazilian Portuguese* (Essex University Department of Language and Linguistics).

Spoken Portuguese (SLS).

Other courses: BBC; Conversaphone; Hugo; Linguaphone; 'Listen and Learn' (Dover); 'Quick and Easy' (Langenscheidt/Hodder); Univerb, Lancashire C.

Phrase-books: Berlitz; Lonely Planet; Pan; Penguin; 'Say it' (in European and Brazilian versions; Dover).

Tuition: *Floodlight*; Hispano and Luso Brazilian Council.

Punjabi Level: 3
An official language of Pakistan and the Indian province of Punjab, it is spoken by some 70 million people in these areas. Two scripts are used: Arabic and Gumurkhi.

Kaur, N.: *Everyday Punjabi* (Weavers Press).
Mavi, B. S.: *Teach Yourself Punjabi* (Mavi Publications). Course book and cassette.
Sharma, J. N. and S. K.: *Punjabi as a Second Language* (Language Centre, Hockley, Birmingham).
Tuition: Bradford and Ilkley Community College; *Floodlight*; International Punjabi Society; SOAS.

Quechua Level: 2
An American Indian language spoken by some 7 million people in Bolivia and Peru.
Cole, P.: *Imbabura Quechua — A Descriptive Grammar* (Routledge).
Phrase-book: Lonely Planet.

Romanian Level: 1
Romanian is a Romance language descended from Latin, and therefore poses no problems for French-, Italian- or Spanish-speakers. It is the mother tongue of 24 million people in Eastern Europe, mainly in Romania.
Murrell, M. and Stefanescu-Draganesti: *Teach Yourself Romanian* (Hodder & Stoughton).
Miroiu, M.: *Romanian Conversation Guide* (Hippocrene).
Deletant, D.: *Colloquial Romanian* (Routledge).
Ilutiu, V.: *Le Roumain sans Peine* (Assimil).
Roceric, A. and Hassing, A. M.: *Romanian Textbook* (Dunwoody).
Spoken Romanian (SLS).
Other course: Conversaphone.
Tuition: *Floodlight*; British-Romanian Friendship Association.

Russian Level: 2
The mother tongue of some 140 million Russians and the second language of 40 million more residents of the former USSR. It is widely used in other countries of Eastern Europe and is an official language of the United Nations.
Russian uses the Cyrillic script, and English-speakers sometimes experience difficulty with the pronunciation and the inflections.
Approach to Russian (National Extension College).
Dawson, C. L. and Humesky, A.: *Modern Russian* (Georgetown University Press). Two volumes.
Fenell, J. L. I.: *The Penguin Russian Course* (Penguin).
Frewin, M.: *Teach Yourself Russian* (Routledge).
Vasilenko, E. and Lamm, E.: *Learn Russian on your Own* (Collets).
Other courses: Amway; Assimil; 'At a Glance' (Barron); BBC; Bilingual; Conversaphone; Hugo; Linguaphone; 'Listen and Learn' (Dover); 'Now You're Talking' (Barron), PILL; 'Quick and Easy' (Langenscheidt/Hodder); SLS; Talking Business (Barron).

Phrase-books: Pan; Penguin; 'Say it' (Dover); Teach Yourself; Vocabulearn.
Tuition: *Floodlight*; Society for Cultural Relations with the CIS; SSEES.
SCR Guide to Russian Classes in the UK (Society for Cultural Relations in the USSR).

Samoan Level: 2
A Polynesian language spoken by some 100,000 people in Western and American Samoa.
  Himkin, G. A. L.: *Samoan Language Course Book* (Polynesian Press, New Zealand). Course book and tape.

Sanskrit Level: 3
An ancient Indian language which is no longer in everyday use but which has had an important influence on many of the languages of India and further afield. Its position is analogous to Latin in Western Europe and it boasts a very rich literature.
  Coulson, M.: *Teach Yourself Sanskrit* (Hodder & Stoughton).
  Tuition: *Floodlight*; Institute of Indian Culture.

Serbo-Croat Level: 2
Serbian and Croatian are essentially the same Slavonic language but with two alphabets: the former using Cyrillic script, the latter Roman for historical reasons. It is spoken by some 18 million people in Bosnia, Croatia and Yugoslavia. Related languages are Slovenian (spoken in Slovenia) and Macedonian (spoken in Macedonia).
  FSI Serbo-Croatian (Audio-Forum). Two volumes and 36 cassettes.
  Welcome — Serbo-Croatian Course for Beginners (Collets).
  Babic, S.: *Serbo-Croatian for Foreigners* (Hipprocrene/Collets).
  Javarek, V. and Sudjic, M.: *Teach Yourself Serbo-Croat* (Hodder & Stoughton).
  Hawkesworth, C.: *Colloquial Serbo-Croat* (Routledge).
  Other courses: Linguaphone; SLS.
  Phrase-books: Berlitz; Conversaphone; Harraps; Hugo; Language 30; 'Say it' (Dover).
  Tuition: *Floodlight*; SSEES.

Shona Level: 2
A Bantu language and one of the major languages of Zimbabwe.
Shona (Audio-Forum). 10 cassettes plus text.
  Dale, D.: *Shona Mini-Companion — A Guide for Beginners* (Mambo Press, PO Box 779, Gweru, Zimbabwe).
  Carter, J. H. and Kahari, G. P.: *Kivurenga Chishóna — An Introductory Shona Reader* (SOAS).
  Munjanje, A. M.: *Everyday Shona and English* (Write and Read Publications, 23 South Avenue, Harare, Zimbabwe).
  Tuition: Africa Centre; SOAS.

Sinhalese Level: 3
The official language of Sri Lanka and mother tongue of some 11 million people. It is one of the Indo-Aryan group of languages (like Hindi) and has its own script.
    FSI Colloquial Sinhalese (Audio-Forum). Two volumes and 34 cassettes.
    Reynolds, C.: *Sinhalese — An Introductory Course* (SOAS).
    Spoken Sinhalese (SLS).
    Phrase-book: Lonely Planet.
    Tuition: SOAS.

Slovenian Level: 2
A Slavonic language closely related to Serbo-Croat spoken in Slovenia.
    Slovene — A Self-Study Course (Collets).
    Jug-Kranjec, H.: *Slovene for Foreigners* (Collets).
    Phrase-book: *Slovene for Travellers* (Collets).
    Tuition: SSEES.

Somali Level: 3
A Semitic language spoken in Somalia.
    Carton Dibeth, V.: *Manuel de Conversation Somali-Français* (Editions Harmattanm 5–7 rue de l'Ecole Polytechnique, 75005 Paris).
    Warner, J.: *Somali Grammar* (Mennonite Board of East Africa, PO Box 14894, Nairobi).
    Issa, A.: *Somali Newspaper Reader* (Dunwoody).
    Zorc, R. D. and Issa, A.: *Somali Textbook* (Dunwoody).
    Tuition: *Floodlight*; SOAS.

Sotho Level: 2
A tonal-click Bantu language spoken in Lesotho, Botswana and South Africa and closely related to Zulu.
    The Language 30 series has short courses in both Northern Sotho and Southern Sotho (Educational Services Corp., Washington).
    Tuition: Africa Centre, SOAS.

Spanish Level: 1
The official language of some 19 countries. There are some 180 million Spanish-speakers in the world — in Spain, much of South America and Central America, Cuba, the Dominican Republic and Puerto Rico, and there is a substantial Spanish-speaking minority in the USA.
    Latin American Spanish differs from the Iberian variety mainly with respect to pronunciation, and there are courses available in both varieties. A Romance language, it presents few difficulties to speakers of French or Italian.
    García Fernández and Sánchez Lobato, J.: *Espanol 2000* (SGEL/European SB).
    Clark, R.: *Mastering Spanish* (Macmillan).
    Halm, W. and Blasco, C.: *Contact Spanish* (Cambridge University Press).

Martín Peres, E.: *Vamos a ver* (EDELSA/European SB).
Patterson, W. R.: *Colloquial Spanish* (Routledge).
Pride, J. C.: *School Spanish Course* (Harper Collins).
Sánchez, A., Ríos, M. and Matilla, J. A.: *Entre nosotros* (SGEL/European SB).
Truscott, S. and Escribano, J.: *Breakthrough Spanish* (Macmillan).
Grimley, M. T. and Herrándiz, P.: *Spanish for Business* (Limitcode).
Kattan-Ibárra, J.: *Teach Yourself Business Spanish* (Hodder & Stoughton).
Lorenzi-Kearon, M. and Kearon, T.: *Medical Spanish* (Audio-Forum). 12 cassettes plus text.
Spanish for the Health Professional (Audio-Forum). 4 cassettes plus text.
Kattan-Ibárra, J. and Connell, T.: *Working with Spanish* (Stanley Thornes).
Connell, T.: *Expo-Spanish* (Stanley Thornes/NIVC). Interactive video course for business people with some knowledge of the language.

Other courses: Accelerated Learning; Amway; Assimil; 'At a Glance' (Barron); Bilingual; Conversaphone; Linguaphone; 'Listen and Learn' (Dover); 'Now You're Talking' (Barron); PILL; 'Quick and Easy' (Langenscheidt/Hodder); Stillitron; Talking Business (Barron); Teach Yourself; Univerb.

Phrase-books: High Pines; Hugo; Pan; Penguin; 'Say it' (Dover); Vocabulearn.

Tuition: *Floodlight*; Spanish Institute.

Swahili Level: 1
A Bantu language influenced by Arabic which is the national language of Tanzania and used widely as a lingua franca in East Africa.

FSI Swahili Basic Course (Audio-Forum). Course book and 20 cassettes.
Adam, H.: *Kiswahili — An Elementary Course* (Helmut Buske, Hamburg).
Haddon, E. B.: *Swahili Lessons* (SOAS).
Mau, J.: *Twende — A Practical Swahili Course* (OUP — Clarendon Press).
Safari, J.: *Swahili Made Easy* (Tanzania Publishing House).
Wilson, P. M.: *Simplified Swahili* (Longman).
Perrott, D. V. and Murphy, J.: *Teach Yourself Swahili* (Hodder & Stoughton).
Spoken Swahili (SLS)
Musyoki, A. and Murphy, J.: *Elementary Swahili Newspaper Reader* (Dunwoody).

Other courses: Conversaphone; Language 30; No-Time.

Phrase-books: Berlitz; Lonely Planet; Say it' (Dover).

Tuition: Africa Centre; Council for African Languages and Culture; *Floodlight*.

Swedish Level: 1
The official language of Sweden and one of the official languages of Finland, Swedish is spoken by some 8 million people in these countries. Closely related to Danish and Norwegian.

McClean, R. J.: *Teach Yourself Swedish* (Hodder & Stoughton).

FSI Swedish Basic Course (Audio-Forum). Course book and 8 cassettes.
Spoken Swedish (SLS).
Other courses: Conversaphone; Language 30; Linguaphone; 'Listen and Learn' (Dover); Teach Yourself; Univerb.
Phrase-books: Berlitz; Pan; 'Say it' (Dover); Vocabulearn.
Tuition: *Floodlight*.

Tamil Level: 3
A member of the Dravidian language group spoken by some 45 million people in the southern Indian state of Tamil Nadu, Sri Lanka and in parts of South-East Asia, East and Southern Africa, and the Caribbean where there are Tamil communities. Tamil has its own alphabet and bears no resemblance at all to Hindi and the northern Indian languages.
Marr, J. R. et al.: *An Introduction to Colloquial Tamil* (SOAS/VSO).
Learn Tamil through English (Read Well Publications, New Delhi).
Vaidyanathan, S. and Murphy, J.: *Tamil Newspaper Reader* (Dunwoody).
Tuition: Institute of Indian Culture; SOAS.

Telugu Level: 3
Like Tamil it is a member of the Dravidian group of languages, and is the official language of the Indian state of Andhra Pradesh in south-eastern India. It is spoken by 55 million people and has its own script.
Spoken Telugu (SLS).
Learn Telugu through English (Read Well Publications, New Delhi).
Tuition: SOAS.

Thai Level: 3
Thai is the national language of Thailand and related to Lao and Shan (spoken in northern Burma). It is tonal and has its own alphabet developed from ancient Indian Languages. Its vocabulary has been enriched by words from Cambodian, Sanskrit and Pali. The language, which is based on the Bangkok dialect, is widely understood throughout the country and in Laos.
FSI Basic Thai (Audio-Forum). Two volumes with 27 cassettes.
Allison, G.: *Easy Thai* (Charles E. Tuttle).
Butori, B. and W.: *Introduction au Thaï* (Assimil).
Bansai and Smith: *Thai in a Week* (Headway Books, Hodder & Stoughton).
Other courses: Conversaphone; Language 30; Linguaphone.
Phrase-books: Lonely Planet; *Spoken Thai* (SLS).
Tuition: SOAS.
Tuition abroad: AUA Language Centre, Rajdamri Road, Bangkok; Union Language Centre, Silom Road, Bangkok.

Tibetan Level: 3
Belonging to the Sino-Tibetan language group, it is the mother tongue of some 5 million people in Tibet and Nepal. Its alphabet is of Indian origin.

Appendix A

Lewin, T. H.: *Manual of Tibetan* (Asian Educational Services, C2/15 Safdarjung Development Area, New Delhi 110016).
Bloomfield, A. and Tshering, Y.: *Tibetan Phrase Book* (Snow Lion Publishing, USA).
Other phrase-books: Lonely Planet.
Tuition: SOAS.

Turkish Level: 2
The official language of Turkey, it is the mother tongue of some 45 million Turks in Turkey itself, in northern Cyprus, in parts of Bulgaria and Greece and in Germany. There are substantial Turkish communities in the UK, the USA and Australia.

The language is one of the Altaic family of languages and is therefore related to Mongolian. It is an agglutinative language with word roots to which several suffixes may be added. Another of its features is vowel harmony whereby in a certain word only certain combinations of vowels may occur. In former times Turkish used the Arabic script, but since Atatürk's language reforms in the 1930s Turkish has been written in the Roman script.

FSI Basic Turkish (Audio-Forum). Two volumes with 25 cassettes.
Hengirmen, M. and Koç, N.: *Türkçe Ögreniyoruz* (Engin Yayinevi, Süleyman Bey Sok 17/11, Maltepe, Ankara).
Lewis, G.: *Teach Yourself Turkish* (Hodder & Stoughton).
Mardin, Y.: *Colloquial Turkish* (Routledge).
Other courses: Conversaphone; 'Get by in'; Language 30; 'Quick and Easy' (Langenscheidt/Hodder).
Murphy, J. and Somay, M.: *Turkish Newspaper Reader* (Dunwoody).
Phrase-books: Berlitz; Hugo; Pan; Penguin; 'Say it' (Dover); Vocabulearn.
Tuition: *Floodlight*; SOAS; Turkish Embassy Education Office.

Twi (Akan) Level: 2
The language of 6 million West Africans resident mainly in southern Ghana. A tonal language, it belongs to the Niger-Congo language group.
FSI Twi Basic Course (Audio-Forum). Course book and 9 cassettes.
Tuition: *Floodlight*; SOAS.

Ukrainian Level: 2
Ukrainian is spoken by some 43 million people in Ukraine and there are estimated to be 600,000 Ukrainian speakers in North America. It is closely related to Russian and written in the Cyrillic script .
Humesky, A.: *Modern Ukrainian* (Canadian Institute of Ukrainian Studies — CIUS).
Struk, D. H.: *Ukrainian for Undergraduates* (CIUS).
Other course: Conversaphone.
Tuition: SSEES.

Urdu Level: 3
The official language of Pakistan and the mother tongue of some 45 million people in both Pakistan and India. It is virtually identical with Hindi, differing only in its script (Arabic) and, to a lesser extent, its vocabulary.
   Urrahman, A.: *Teach Yourself Urdu in Two Months* (Hippocrene).
   Malik, P.: *Spoken Urdu* (Urdu Language Development Board, 16 Bream Avenue, Solihull, West Midlands B26 1JS).
   Mavi, B. S.: *Teach Yourself Urdu* (Mavi Publications). Course book and cassettes.
   Russell, R.: *A New Course in Urdu and Spoken Hindi for Learners in Britian* (SOAS).
   Learn Urdu through English (Read Well Publications, New Delhi).
   Ahmad, M.: *Urdu Newspaper Reader* (Dunwoody).
   Other courses: Teach Yourself; SLS; Lancashire C.
   Phrase-book: Lonely Planet.
   Tuition: *Floodlight*; SOAS; Institute of Indian Culture.
   Hindi Urdu Guide (BBC Education).

Vietnamese Level: 3
The national language of Vietnam is spoken by some 50 million people, including Vietnamese communities in Europe, Australasia and the USA. A tonal language, it is written in Roman script devised by Alexandre de Rhodes, a French missionary, which makes extensive use of accents.
   FSI Basic Vietnamese (Audio-Forum). Two volumes with 32 cassettes.
   Read Vietnamese (Charles E. Tuttle, Tokyo).
   Speak Vietnamese (Charles E. Tuttle, Tokyo).
   Le Vietnamien sans Peine (Assimil).
   Spoken Vietnamese (SLS).
   Other courses: Conversaphone; Language 30.
   Phrase-books: Nguyen Dinh Hoa; *Vietnamese Phrase Book* (Charles E. Tuttle).
   Tuition: *Floodlight*; SOAS.

Welsh Level: 2
The oldest language in the British Isles spoken by about 400,000 people in the western extremities of Wales. Welsh is experiencing something of a comeback and apart from having official status is being increasingly used in schools thoughout the Principality. Although an Indo-European language, its structure is quite different from that of English, and one of its features is an elaborate system of mutations (changes) to initial consonants.
   Approach to Welsh (National Extension College). Correspondence course with cassettes.
   Davies, B.: *Catchphrase — A Course in Spoken Welsh* (Sain Ricordiaw Cyf, Llanwrog, Caernarfon, Gwynedd. Tel: (0286) 831111.
   Finch, P. (ed): *How to Learn Welsh* (Davies).

Gruffudd, H.: *Welsh is Fun* (Lolfa).
James, D. L. and Davies, C.: *A Conversational Welsh Course — Cwrs Cymraeg Llafar* (Davies).
James, D. L.: *A Crash Course in Welsh — Cwrs Carlam Cymraeg* (Davies).
Jones, R. M.: *Welsh for Adults* (University of Wales Press) Three vols.
Philip Davies, J.: *Cloucian — Beginners' Course in Welsh* (Language Unit, North-East Wales Institute of Higher Education, Kelsterton Road, Cannah's Quay, Deeside, Clwyd CH4 4BR).
Wilkes, A.: *Welsh for Beginners* (Usborne).
Rhys Jones, T.: *Teach Yourself Welsh* (Hodder & Stoughton).
Other courses: BBC; Linguaphone.
Phrase-books: *Get Around in Welsh* (Celtic).
Tuition: *Floodlight*; Welsh Language Society; Welsh Learners' Council; Welsh Joint Education Committee.

Xhosa Level: 2
A tonal language belonging to the Niger Congo group of languages spoken by 5.3 million people in Southern Africa.
Courses: Language 30.
Tuition: SOAS.

Yiddish Level: 1
A Germanic language with Hebrew, Romance and Slavonic elements spoken by Jews in Israel, the USA, South America and the USSR.
Kogos, F.: *Instant Yiddish* (Citadel Press, USA).
Other courses: Conversaphone; Language 30.
Phrase-books: 'Say it' (Dover).
Tuition: Africa Centre; CILT; *Floodlight*.

Yoruba Level: 2
A language belonging to the Kwa group spoken by some 18 million people in southern Nigeria.
Barber, A.: *A Beginner's Course in Yoruba* (New Horn Press, Nigeria).
Rowlands, E.: *Teach Yourself Yoruba* (Hodder & Stoughton).
FSI Yoruba Basic Course (Audio-Forum). Course book and 36 cassettes.
Tuition: Africa Centre; *Floodlight*; SOAS.

Zulu Level: 2
A tonal Bantu language spoken by some 5.5 million people in southern Africa.
Taljaard, P. C. and Bosch, S. E.: *Handbook of Isizulu* (J. L. van Schaik, Libri Building, Church Street, Pretoria, South Africa).
Other courses: Language 30; Language Learn.
Tuition: Africa Centre; *Floodlight*; SOAS.

Appendix B
Language Course Publishers and Distributors

Course Price Guide: A — around £15 ($25) or less; B — £15 ($25) to £40 ($60); C — over £40 ($60).

Accelerated Learning Systems, Uni-Vite House, 50 Aylesbury Road, Aston Clinton, Aylesbury, Bucks HP22 5AH. Tel: (0296) 631177.
    Courses in French, German, Italian and Spanish with 12 cassettes, manuals and video learning to Waystage level. (C)

Accent Educational Publishers, 17 Isbourne Way, Winchcombe, Glos. GL54 5NS. Tel: (0242) 604480.
    Distributors of language books mainly for schools for EMC (USA) and CIS Educational (Australia). Publishers of the popular Italian course for adults 'Sempre Avanti'. (A)

Amway (UK) Ltd, Snowdon Drive, Milton Keynes MK6 1AR
    Distributors of the AAC 7000 language learning system developed by Philips for French, Dutch, German, Italian, Japanese, Russian, Spanish. The package consists of a minilab, 18 cassettes, 3 picture books, 3 workbooks, 3 multilingual textbooks. (C)

Appletree Press Ltd, 7 James Street South, Belfast BT2 8DL. Tel: (0232) 243074.

Assimil, 13 rue Gay-Lussac, BP 25, 94431 Chennevières/Marne, France.
    Distributor: Silco, 7 Russell Gardens, London NW11 9NJ. Tel: (081) 458 6478.
    Publishers of courses in Arabic, Dutch, French, German, Italian, Russian and Spanish for speakers of English. There is a wider range of language courses available for French-speakers including Breton, Creole, Corsican, Hungarian and Vietnamese. Two to four cassettes accompany each course. (B)

'At a Glance' series: see Barron's.

Audio-Forum, Microworld House, 2–6 Foscope Mews, London W9 2HH. Tel: (071) 266 2202; also Suite LA 40, 96 Broad Street, Guilford CT 06437, USA).
    Distributors and publishers of a wide range of language materials, notably the United States Foreign Service Institute courses. Languages: Afrikaans, Amharic, Arabic, Armenian, Bulgarian, Burmese, Cambodian, Chinese, Creole, Czechoslovak, Danish, Dutch, Finnish, French, Fula, German, Greek, Hausa, Hebrew, Hindi, Hungarian, Icelandic, Indonesian, Irish, Italian, Japanese, Korean, Latin, Latvian, Malay,

Norwegian, Persian, Pilipino, Polish, Portuguese, Romanian, Russian, Serbo-Croat, Sinhalese, Sotho (Northern and Southern), Spanish, Shona, Swahili, Swedish, Telugu, Thai, Turkish, Twi, Urdu, Vietnamese, Welsh, Xhosa, Yiddish, Yoruba and Zulu. (ABC)

Authentik, O'Reilly Institute, Trinity College, Dublin 2. Tel: Dublin 77512.

Publishers of newspapers and cassettes for learners of French, German and Spanish. (A)

Barron's Educational Series Inc.: 256 Wireless Boulevard, Happauge, NY 11788.

Distributor: D Services, Euston Street, Freeman's Common, Leicester LE2 7SS. Tel: (0533) 547671.

Publishers of the 'At a Glance' series of phrase-books. Languages: Arabic, Chinese, French, German, Korean, Italian, Japanese, Russian and Spanish.

Also 'Learn the Fast and Fun Way' series: French, German, Italian and Spanish.

Also 'Master the Basics' series: French, German, Italian, Spanish.

Also 'Now You're Talking' series: Arabic, Chinese, French, German, Italian, Japanese, Russian, Spanish (book and cassette).

Also 'Talking Business' series: French, German, Italian, Japanese, Korean, Spanish. (A)

BBC (British Broadcasting Corporation), Woodlands, 80 Wood Lane, London W12 0TT. Tel: (081) 576 2237.

The BBC broadcasts a number of TV and radio language courses and most of their published courses are designed to be used in conjunction with these. For details of current broadcasting plans and residential language courses based on BBC series you should contact BBC Education Information, London W5 2PA. Tel: (081) 991 8031.

Publishes the 'Get by in . . .' series consisting of a course book and cassettes. Languages: Arabic, Chinese, French, German, Greek, Italian, Hindi Urdu, Japanese, Portuguese, Serbo-Croat, Spanish, Turkish. (A) Video courses available for French, German, Spanish and Italian.

Also 'Language and People' series: Greek, Russian, Japanese.

Also video courses 'A vous la France', 'Buongiorno Italia', 'Italianissimo', 'Deutsch Direkt', 'España Viva', 'Etoiles' 'Japanese Language and People'. Also — for people with some basic knowledge — 'French/German/Spanish Means Business' (C)

Also phrase books for German, Italian and Spanish. (A)

Berlitz, Avenue d'Ouchy 61, 1000 Lausanne 6, Switzerland.

Distributor: Charles Letts & Co. Ltd, Diary House, Borough Road, London SE1 1DW. Tel: (071) 407 8891. Publishers of the 'Berlitz for Travellers' and the 'Berlitz 90' series of language phrase-books which cover Arabic, Chinese, Danish, Dutch, French, German, Greek, Hebrew, Hungarian, Italian, Japanese, Norwegian, Polish, Portuguese, Russian, Serbo-Croat, Spanish, Latin American Spanish, Swahili, Turkish. There are cassettes to accompany the books. Berlitz also publish the 'Berlitz European Phrase Book' covering some 14 European languages. (A)

Also Berlitz videos for travellers: French, German, Italian (B); and Reader's Digest/Berlitz 'On the move' for French consisting of 4 cassettes, phrase-book and country guide. (C)

The cassette-based Berlitz Basic Home Study course (C) and Express Course (B) are available for French, German, Italian and Spanish.

Bilingual Books Inc., Sunset Publishing Corporation, 80 Willow Road, Menlo Park, CA 94025-3691, USA (ISBN 0-944502).

Distributor: Ruskin Book Services, Marlborough House, Marlborough Street, Kidderminster DY10 1BJ. Tel: (0562) 515151.

Publishers of the '10 Minutes a Day' language series designed to help the business traveller or tourist develop a basic conversational ability in a foreign language. 128 pages; illustrated in colour. Languages: Chinese, French, German, Hebrew, Italian, Japanese, Norwegian, Russian, Spanish. (A)

Bond Street Music, 5 Wigmore Street, London W1H 9LA. Tel: (071) 491 4117.

Distributors of a wide range of language courses.

Helmut Buske, Friedrichsgaberweg 138, Postfach 1249, 2000 Norderstadt, Germany.

Cambridge University Press, The Edinburgh Building, Shaftesbury Road, Cambridge CB2 2RU. Tel: (0223) 312393.

Canadian Institute of Ukrainian Studies.

Distributor: Orbis Books Ltd, 66 Kenway Road, London SW5 ORD. Tel: (071) 370 2210.

CD–I Training Ltd, Freeland House, Station Road, Dorking, Surrey RH4 1UL; Tel: (0306) 875777. Fax: (0306) 875789.

Interactive training packages.

Central Institute of Indian Languages, Manasagangokri, Mysore, India.

Collets, Denington Estate, Wellingborough, Northants NN8 2QT. Tel: (0933) 224351.

Publishers and distributors of a wide range of language books. Eastern European languages are their speciality. Bookshops at 129–131 Charing Cross Road, London WC2H 0EQ and 40 Great Russell Street, London WC1B 3PJ.

'Colloquial . . .' series: see Routledge.

Comput–Ed Ltd, Long Lane, Dawlish, Devon EX7 0QR. Tel: (0626) 866247. Fax: (0626) 867248.

Distributors of language training video cassettes.

Conversaphone, 1 Comac Loop, Rouconkoma, NY, USA.

Distributor: LCL, 104 Judd Street, London WC1. Tel: (071) 837 0486.

Publishes Modern Method language courses for French, German, Italian, Portuguese, Russian, Spanish, Swedish (2 course books accompanied by 2 cassettes).

Also 'Round the World Languages' and 'Languages 5000' for Afrikaans,

Arabic, Bulgarian, French, Czech, German, Greek, Hindi, Indonesian, Irish, Italian, Japanese, Korean, Lithuanian, Malay, Persian, Pilipino (Tagalog), Romanian, Russian, Serbo-Croat, Spanish, Swahili, Swedish, Thai, Turkish, Ukrainian, Vietnamese, Yiddish. These are phrasebooks accompanied by cassettes or records. (AB)

Cork University Press, University College, Cork, Ireland.

Christopher Davies, PO Box 403, Swansea SA2 9BE. Tel: (0792) 48825.

Dover Publications Inc.: 31 East Street, Mineola, NY 11501, USA.
Distributor: Constable & Co. Ltd, The Lanchesters, 162 Fulham Palace Road, London W6 9ER. Tel: (081) 741 3663.

Publishers of the 'Listen and Learn' series comprising a course book and records/cassettes. Languages: French, German, Modern Greek, Modern Hebrew, Italian, Japanese, Portuguese, Russian, Spanish, Swedish. (AB)

Also the 'Essential Grammar' series: Dutch, French, German, Modern Greek, Italian, Japanese, Portuguese, Spanish. (A)

Also the 'Say It' series of phrase-books: Egyptian Arabic, Chinese, Czech, Danish, Dutch, Finnish, French, German, Modern Greek, Modern Hebrew, Hindi, Hungarian, Indonesian, Italian, Japanese, Norwegian, Polish, Portuguese, Brazilian Portuguese, Russian, Serbo-Croat, Latin American Spanish, Swahili, Swedish, Turkish, Yiddish. (A)

Other language courses in the Dover catalogue: Chinese, Turkish.

Richard Drew Publishing, 6 Clairmont Gardens, Glasgow G3 7LW. Tel: (041) 333 9341.

Publishes the 'Travelmate' series of phrase-books for French, German, Greek, Italian, Japanese, Portuguese and Spanish. Also 'The German Businessmate' — a phrase-book for business people. (A)

Dunwoody Press, PO Box 1825, Wheaton, Maryland 20915, USA.
Distributor: LCL, 104 Judd Street, London WC1H 9NF. (C)

Early Advantage, MBI, Inc, Cox Lane, Chessington, Surrey KT9 1SE. Tel: (081) 391 2291.

Distributors of *The BBC Language Course for Children*: French, German, Italian, Spanish video and audio cassettes with activity book, story book and parents' handbook. (C)

Educational Services Corporation, 1725 K Street NW No. 408, Washington DC 20006.
Distributor: Audio-Forum, Microworld House, 2–6 Foscope Mews, London W9 2HH. Tel: (071) 266 2202.

Publishers of the 'Language 30' phrase-book series.

European Schoolbooks Ltd, Ashville Trading Estate, The Runnings, Cheltenham GL51 9PQ. Tel: (0242) 245252. London showroom: The European Bookshop, 4 Regent Place, Warwick Street, London W1R 6BH. Tel: (071) 734 5259.

Publisher and distributor of a wide range of French, German and Spanish books and magazines including language manuals for adults from Continental publishers. UK representative for CLE International,

Hachette Classiques, Hatier of France; Heyne Huber, Kessler Verlag, Klett, Langenscheidt, Ullstein Verlag of Germany; Colegio de Espana, EDELSA, SGEL of Spain.

Foreign Service Institute, US State Department, Washington DC, USA.
Audio-Forum, Microworld House, 2–6 Foscope Mews, London W9 2HH. Tel: (071) 266 2202.

Self-study courses with cassettes developed for US diplomats. Languages: Amharic, Arabic (Saudi Arabian), Bulgarian, Cambodian (Khmer), Chinese (Cantonese), French, German, Greek, Hausa, Hebrew, Japanese, Korean, Portuguese, Serbo-Croat, Spanish, Swahili, Swedish, Thai, Turkish, Vietnamese, Yoruba, Zulu. (C)

Gairm Publications, 29 Waterloo Street, Glasgow G2 6BZ. Tel: (041) 221 1971.

'Get by in . . .' series: see BBC.

Mary Glasgow Publications, Old Station Drive, Leckhampton, Cheltenham GL53 0DN. Tel: (0242) 584429.

Publishers of French, German and Spanish language courses principally for use in schools as well as language magazines at different levels of competence.

Gloview Co Ltd, 2–60–6 Nihonbashi-Hamucho, Chuo-ku, Tokyo 103, Japan.

Distributor: Academic and University Publishers Group, 1 Gower Street, London WC1 6EA. Tel: (071) 724 7577.

Guildsoft, Wentworth House, Dormy Avenue, Mannamead, Plymouth PL3 5BE. Tel: (0752) 251155.

Distributors of Traveler's Guild language software (French, German, English, Japanese). Also Hyperglot software (Chinese, French, German, Russian, Spanish). (C)

Harper Collins, 77–85 Fulham Palace Road, Hammersmith, London W6 8JB. Tel: (081) 741 7070.

Publishers of a range of language dictionaries, school textbooks (under the Collins Educational imprint and the 'Traveller' series of phrasebooks in French, German, Greek, Italian, Portuguese. (A)

Harrap Publishing Group Ltd, 43–45 Annandale Street, Edinburgh EH7 4AZ. Tel: (031) 557 4571.

Publish a series of phrase-books for Chinese, Czech, German, Hungarian, Italian, Polish, Russian, Serbo-Croat, Spanish, Turkish. (Some also available packaged with a cassette in the 'Essential' series.) (A)

Also 'Jiffy' phrase-books for French, German, Italian, Spanish (also available with cassette). (A)

Also 'Everyday Japanese'.

Also 'Drive in . . .' French, German, Italian, Spanish including cassettes. (B)

Heinemann Educational, Halley Court, Jordan Hill, Oxford OX2 8EJ. Tel: (0865) 311366.

Most of Heinemann's language books are for school use, but 'Allez-y' has been used successfully with adult classes.

High Pines Press, PO Box 42, Reigate, Surrey RH2 8YW.
Publishers of the Speak Easy Phrasemaker phrase-books for French, German and Italian. (A)

Hippocrene Books Inc., 171 Madison Avenue, New York, NY 10016.
Distributor: Gazelle Book Services, Falcon House, Queen Square, Lancaster LA1 1RN. Tel: (0524) 68765. (A)

Hodder & Stoughton Ltd, Mill Road, Dunton Green, Sevenoaks, Kent TN13 2YA. Tel: (0732) 450111.
Publishers of the extensive 'Teach Yourself' series of language courses for many of which cassettes are available (marked with an asterisk). Languages: Afrikaans, Arabic*, Catalan, Chinese (Cantonese), Chinese (Mandarin)*, Czech, Danish, Dutch, Esperanto*, Finnish, French*, Business French*, Gaelic, German*, Greek, Ancient Greek, Modern Greek, New Testament Greek, Hausa, Biblical Hebrew, Hindi*, Icelandic, Indonesian, Irish, Italian*, Japanese*, Latin, Maltese, Norwegian, Modern Persian, Polish, Portuguese*, Romanian, Russian, Sanskrit, Serbo-Croat, Spanish*, Business Spanish*, Swahili, Swedish, Turkish*, Welsh*, Yoruba. (AB)

Also publishers of the Headway 'In your Pocket' phrase-books for French, German, Italian and Spanish and distributors of the Langenscheidt 'Quick and Easy' language travel packs for French, German, Greek, Italian, Japanese, Portuguese, Russian, Spanish, Turkish. (A)

Also publishes under the Headway imprint the 'In a Week' series for French, German, Greek, Italian, Japanese, Portuguese, Spanish, Thai. (A)

Holt, Rinehart & Winston, 24–28 Oval Road, London NW1 7DX. Tel: (071) 267 4466.

HS Promotions, 15A Cantelowes Road, London NW1 9XP. Tel: (081) 761 6566.
Distributors of language learning games.

Hugo's Language Books, Old Station Yard, Marlesford, Woodbridge, Suffolk IP13 0AG. Tel: (0728) 746546.
The 'Three Months' series is available either as a separate course book or as a course book accompanied by four cassettes. Languages: Dutch, French, German, Greek, Italian, Japanese (Simplified), Norwegian, Portuguese, Russian, Swedish, Turkish, Spanish. (A)
Also Hugo Travel Packs consisting of a phrase-book plus one cassette are available for most of the above languages plus Arabic, Danish and Thai. Phrase-books are also available separately.
Also 'At the wheel' audio courses for French, German, Italian and Spanish. (B)
Also French/German for Business with cassettes. (C)

Kodansha International, 17–14 Otowa 1-chome, Bunkyo-ku, Tokyo 112.
Distributor: Biblios, Star Road, Partridge Green, Horsham, West Sussex RH13 8LD. Tel: (0403) 3710971.

Kuperard (London) Ltd, 9 Hampstead West, 224 Iverson Road, West

Hampstead, London NW6 2HL. Tel: (071) 372 4722

    Publish and distribute books on Hebrew.

Lancashire College, Southport Road, Chorley, Lancs PR7 1NB. Tel: (0257) 276719.

    Publishers of open learning courses, many with a business orientation, for Chinese, Danish, Dutch, French, German, Hungarian, Italian, Japanese, Norwegian, Portuguese, Spanish, Urdu. (C) Also 60-minute business videos for French, German and Spanish.

Langenscheidt AG, Neuserstrasse, Munich, Germany.

    Distributor: European Schoolbooks Ltd, Ashville Trading Estate, The Runnings, Cheltenham GL51 9PQ. Tel: (0242) 245252.

'Language and People' series: see BBC.

Language Learn, Audio Word Pty Ltd, PO Box 17530, Hillbrow 2038, South Africa.

    Publishers of Afrikaans and Zulu courses. Available from Audio Forum.

Language 30: see Educational Services Corporation.

Languages Information Centre, 32 Stryd Ebeneser, Pontypridd, Mid Glamorgan CF37 5PB. Tel: (0443) 492243.

LCL, 104 Judd Street, London WC1H 9NF. Tel: (071) 837 0487.

    Distributors of Conversaphone and Univerb courses. Stock courses in the following languages: Afrikaans, Albanian, Amharic, Arabic, Armenian, Baluchi, Bengali, Breton, Bulgarian, Burmese, Cambodian, Catalan, Chinese, Chinyanga, Cornish, Czech, Danish, Egbo, Esperanto, Finnish, French, Fula, Gaelic, German, Greek, Gujarati, Hausa, Hebrew, Hindi, Hungarian, Icelandic, Ibo, Indonesian, Irish, Italian, Japanese, Kikuyu, Kirundi, Kiswahili, Kituba, Kongo, Korean, Kurdish, Lao, Latin, Lithuanian, Maori, Malay, Mende, Mptu, Nepali, Norwegian, Occitan, Persian, Pidgin, Pilipino, Polish, Portuguese, Punjabi, Romanian, Russian, Serbo-Croat, Shona, Sinhalese, Siswati, Somali, Sotho, Spanish, Swahili, Swedish, Tamil, Telugu, Thai, Tonga, Tswana, Turkish, Twi, Ukrainian, Urdu, Vietnamese, Welsh, Xhosa, Yiddish, Yoruba, Zulu. (ABC)

Learning Centre, The Stables, 17 Church Street, Oadby, Leicester LE2 5DB. Tel: (0533) 710439.

    Distributors of the BBC/Vektor/IBM inter-active language courses on laser video discs in French, German and Spanish.

Limitcode Ltd, Tatton Buildings, 6 Old Hall Road, Gatley, Cheadle, Cheshire SK8 4BE. Tel: (061) 428 3000.

    Publishers of 'French/German/Spanish for Business', each a 120-hour course split into 3 stages with taped and other materials; also 'French for Receptionists'. Not really suitable for self-study. (C)

Linguaphone Institute Ltd, St Giles House, 50 Poland Street, London W1V 4AX. Tel: (071) 734 0574.

    Standard courses consisting of study and exercise books and either 4, 6 or 10 cassettes in Afrikaans, Arabic, Chinese, Danish, Dutch, Finnish, French, Greek, Hebrew, Hindi, Icelandic, Indonesian, Irish Gaelic,

Japanese, Korean, Malay, Norwegian, Polish, Portuguese, Russian, Serbo-Croat, Spanish, Swedish, Thai, Welsh. (C)
Specialist business courses with 16 cassettes, course books and mini-lab in: Arabic, Chinese, French, German, Italian, Russian, Spanish, Swedish. (C)

'Listen and Learn' series: see Dover.

Lolfa, Hen Swyddfa'r Heddlu, Talybont, Dyfed SY24 5HE. Tel: (097) 086 304.

Lonely Planet, PO Box 617, Hawthorn, Victoria 3122, Australia.
Distributors: Roger Lascelles, 47 York Road, Brentford, Middlesex TW8 0QP. Tel: (081) 847 0935 and Embarcadero West, 112 Linden Street, Oakland, CA 94607, USA.
This guidebook publisher now has an interesting range of phrase-books mainly for Asian languages. (A)

Longman Group Ltd, Burnt Mill, Harlow, Essex CM20 2JE. Tel: (0279) 26721.
Survive Travelpacks. Languages: French, German, Greek. (A)

Macmillan Education, Brunel Road, Houndsmills, Basingstoke, Hants RG21 2XS. Tel: (0256) 29242.
Publishers of the Breakthrough series of business language courses each consisting of a course book and 3 cassettes. Languages: French, German, Greek, Italian, Spanish.
Also 'The Master Series' for Arabic, French, German, Spanish, Italian, Japanese (A) for which cassettes are also available. (B)

Magic Marketing Ltd, 39 Alston Drive, Bradwell Abbey, Milton Keynes MK13 9HA. Tel: (0908) 321321.
Publishers of the Paul Daniels Magic Memory Method courses: French, German, Spanish. (B)

Managed Learning, Westminster College, Harcourt Hill, North Hinksey, Oxford OX2 9AS. Tel: (0865) 798188.
Publishers of French, German, Italian and Spanish language training materials for business and the tourist industry. Suitable for self-study. (C)

Mavi Publications, 465 Sutton Road, Walsall WS5 3AU. Tel: (0922) 29102.

Mercier Press, PO Box 5, 4 Bridge Street, Cork, Ireland. Tel: Cork 504022.

Nagra and Nagra, 399 Ansty Road, Coventry CV2 3BQ. Tel: (0203) 617314.

National Extension College (NEC), 18 Broadlands Avenue, Cambridge CB2 2HN. Tel: (0223) 316644.

Thomas Nelson and Sons Ltd, Nelson House, Mayfield Road, Walton-on Thames, Surrey KT12 5PL. Tel: (0932) 246133.
Most Nelson language books are school oriented, but the Italian course 'Ciao' is suitable for adults. Also publishers of video and audio cassette materials to supplement courses and distributors of European Language Institute magazines. (A)

Nentori Publishing House, Albania.
  Distributors: Parfitts Book Services, 15 Barley Close, Warminster, Wiltshire BA12 9LX. Tel: (0985) 216371.
New Horn Press, POB 1533, Ibadan, Nigeria.
  Distributor: African Books Collective, The Jam Factory, 27 Park End Street, Oxford OX1 1HU. Tel: (0865) 726686.
'Now You're Talking' series: see Barron's.
Oleander Press, 17 Stansgate Avenue, Cambridge CB2 2QZ.
  Publishes books on Friulan, Romagnol, and Romontsch.
Oxford University Press, Walton Street, Oxford OX2 6DP. Tel: (0865) 56767.
  Publishers of several language courses for schools and the 'Just for Business' learning packages which comprise 3 cassettes and a course book. Languages: French, German, Italian, Spanish. (B)
Pan Books Ltd, Hamilton Close, Houndsmill Industrial Estate, Basingstoke, Hants. Tel: (0256) 464481.
  Publishers of the 'Travellers' phrase-book series. Languages: Greek, Italian, Japanese, Portuguese, Russian, Spanish, Scandinavian languages (Danish, Norwegian, Swedish), Turkish. (A)
Papaloizos Inc.
  Distributor: Zeno Publishers, 4 Denmark Street, London WC2H 8LP. Tel: (071) 836 2522.
Penguin Books Ltd, Bath Road, Harmondsworth, Middlesex UB7 0DA. Tel: (081) 759 1984.
  Publishers of phrase-books for French, Greek, Portuguese, Russian, Spanish, Turkish. Also the 'Penguin Russian Course'. (A)
Penton Overseas Inc.: 2091 Las Palmas Drive, Suite A, Carlsbad, CA 92009, USA.
  Publishers of the Vocabulearn series of phrase-books for Armenian, French, Chinese, Italian, Japanese, Korean, Russian, Spanish, Swedish. (A)
PILL (Programmed Instruction Language Learning), World of Learning (Bristol) Ltd, Springfield House, West Street, Bedminster, Bristol BS3 3NX. Tel: (0272) 639159.
  Self-instructional course with book, 4 cassettes and guide to letter-writing etiquette. Languages: French, German, Italian, Spanish. (C)
Pitman Publishing, 128 Long Acre, London WC2E 9AN. Tel: (071) 379 7383 and Slaidburn Crescent, Southport PR9 9YF.
  Publishers in collaboration with the BBC, Open University, Department of Industry and Eurotunnel of two multi-media training packages for business French and German. Some prior knowledge of the language is assumed. (C)
Polynesian Press, PO Box 47–267, Ponsonby, New Zealand.
Read Well Publications, PO Box 6574, Delhi 110027, India.
  Publishers of the 'Learn through English' series for a number of Indian languages including Assamese, Bengali, Hindi, Kannada, Maharati, Malayalam, Oriya, Tamil, Telugu, Urdu. (A)

Appendix B

Reader's Digest Association, 25 Berkeley Square, London W1X 6AB. Tel: (071) 629 8144.
> Distributor: Charles Letts & Co. Ltd, Thorneybank Industrial Estate, Dalkeith, Midlothian EH22 2NE. Tel: (031) 663 1971.
> 'At home with' series of courses for French, German, Italian and Spanish: 16 cassettes, no textbook. (C)

Rolnik Publishers, Israel.
> Distributor: Kuperard, 30 Cliff Road, London NW1 9AG. Tel: (071) 284 0512.

Routledge, 11 New Fetter Lane, London EC4P 4EE. Tel: (071) 583 9855.
> Publishers of the 'Colloquial' series of language courses for which cassettes are available. Languages: Albanian, Arabic, Chinese, Czech, Dutch, French, German, Greek, Hungarian, Italian, Japanese, Persian, Polish, Portuguese, Romanian, Russian, Serbo-Croat, Spanish, Swedish, Turkish. (AB)

Ruposhi Bangla, 220 Tooting High Street, London SW17 0SG. Tel: (081) 672 7843.
> Publishers and distributors of 'Learning Bengali', 'Bengali for Foreigners', 'Bengali Self-Taught' and 'Learn Bengali Yourself'. Also acts as an advice centre for students of Bengali. (AB)

Sain (Recordiaw) Cyf, Llandwrog, Caernarfon, Gwynedd. Tel: (0268) 831111.

'Say it' series: see Dover.

School of Oriental and African Studies (SOAS), Publications Department, Thornhaugh Street, Russell Square, London WC1H OXG. Tel: (071) 637 2388.
> Publishers of a number of courses for African and Oriental languages developed in-house. Some of the courses developed in-house are not listed in the SOAS catalogue. Cassettes are available on application to SOAS to accompany most course books. (ABC)

Snow Line Publications, PO Box 6483, Ithaca, NY 14851, USA.
> Distributor: Element Books, Longmead, Shaftesbury, Dorset SP7 8PL. Tel: (0747) 51339.

Sodaney Publishers, PO Box 618, London SW8 4JN.

Spoken Language Services, PO Box 783, Ithaca, NY 12850.
> Distributor: Silco, 7 Russell Gardens, London NW11 9NJ. Tel: (081) 458 6478.
> Course books usually accompanied by around six cassettes for Albanian, Amharic, Armenian, Burmese, Chinese (Taiwanese and Amoy-Hokkien), Danish, Dutch, Finnish, French, German, Hausa, Hebrew, Hindi, Hungarian, Indonesian, Italian, Japanese, Korean, Malay, Norwegian, Persian, Pilipino (Tagalog), Polish, Portuguese, Russian, Serbo-Croat, Sinhalese, Swahili, Swedish, Telugu, Thai, Urdu, Vietnamese. (B)

Stillit Books, 72 New Bond Street, London W1Y 0QY. Tel: (071) 493 1177.
> Publishers of the Stillitron range of minilab courses for French, German,

Italian and Spanish. (C)
Summer Institute of Linguistics, Horsleys Green, High Wycombe, Bucks HP14 3XL.
Stanley Thornes (Publishers) Ltd, Old Station Drive, Leckhampton, Cheltenham, Glos GL53 0DN. Tel: (0242) 584429.
> Publishers of a number of language courses for Dutch, French, German, Italian, Russian and Spanish mainly for use in schools. Some of the business courses, notably the 'Working with' series, are suitable for adults. (A)

Tanzania Publishing House.
> Distributor: Africa Books Collective Ltd, The Jam Factory, 27 Park End Street, Oxford OX1 1HU. Tel: (0865) 726686.

Times Editions Pte Ltd, Times Centre, 1 New Industrial Road, Singapore 1953.
> Distributor: Pandemic Ltd, 71 Great Russell Street, London WC1B 3BN. Tel: (071) 242 3298.
> Publishers of a number of course books and phrase-books for Malay and Indonesian. (A)

'Travelmate' series: see Drew.
Truran Publications, Trewolsta, Trewirgie Hill, Redruth, Cornwall TR15 2TB. Tel: (0209) 216796.
Charles E. Tuttle Co. Inc., 2–6 Suido 1-chome, Bunkyo-ku, Tokyo, Japan 112; 28 South Main Street, Rutland, Vermont, USA.
> Distributor: Simon & Schuster International Group, West Garden Place, Kendal Street, London W2 2AQ. Tel: (071) 724 7577.
> Mainly East Asian language books. (AB)

University of Hawaii Press.
> Distributor: Academic and University Publishers Group, 1 Gower Street, London WC1E 6HA. Tel: (071) 636 6005. (A)

University Press of America.
> Distributor: International Book Distributors, 66 Wood Lane End, Hemel Hempstead HP2 4RG. Tel: (0442) 231555.

Usborne Publishing, Usborne House, 83–85 Saffron Hill, London EC1N 8RT.
> Distributor: D. Services, 6 Euston Street, Freeman's Common, Aylestone Road, Leicester LE2 7SS. Tel: (0533) 547671.
> Publishers of a number of colourfully illustrated language books for children aged 8 upwards. The '... for Beginners' series consists of introductory books in French, German, Irish, Italian, Spanish and Welsh, and there are also Guides to French, German, Italian and Spanish for young people. Cassettes are available for some of the books. (A)

Vocabulearn: see Penton.
Weaver Publications, Tregeraint House, Zennor, St. Ives, Cornwall TR26 3DB. Tel: (0736) 797061.
Wida Software Ltd, 2 Nicholas Gardens, London W5 5HY. Tel: (081) 567 6941.

Distributors and publishers of computer-assisted language learning programmes for a limited number of European languages. These are not really appropriate for unsupervised self-study.
Wie und Wo Verlag, Postfach 2464, D5300 Bonn 1.
Publishers of language school directories: 'Learning Languages', 'Learning French', 'Learning Spanish', 'Learning German'.
Yale University Press, 23 Pond Street, London NW3 2PN. Tel: (071) 431 4422. (AB)

HOW TO LIVE & WORK IN GERMANY
Nessa Loewenthal

Whether you are planning to relocate for three months or three years, this is the book for you. It covers such practical topics as entry requirements, transportation, money matters, housing, schools, insurance and much besides. It also includes valuable pointers to German values, customs, business practices and etiquette to help you make the most of your stay. Nessa Loewenthal is Director of Trans Cultural Services, and a consultant specialising in intercultural briefing. 'Detailed help is given on how to find work in Germany including... a comprehensive list of organisations which offer the chance to combine the experience of living in Germany with a useful activity.' *Phoenix/Association of Graduate Careers Advisory Services.*

£7.99, 142pp illus. 1 85703 006 0.

Please add postage & packing (UK £1.00 per copy. Europe £2.00 per copy. World £3.00 per copy airmail).
How To Books Ltd, Plymbridge House, Estover Road, Plymouth PL6 7PZ, United Kingdom. Tel: (0752) 695745. Fax: (0752) 695699. Telex: 45635.

Appendix C
Useful Addresses: Course Providers and Miscellaneous

Aberdeen College of Commerce, Hoburn Street, Aberdeen AB9 2YT. Tel: (0224) 572611. Language training.

ACCENT: The Association of Centres for Excellence in Foreign Language Training, c/o OMTRAC, The Clock House, North Street, Midhurst, West Sussex. Tel: (0730) 815726.

Accents Language and Leisure, BP 01510 Artemare, France. Tel: Manchester (061) 798 0388. Residential French languages courses in France.

Africa Centre. Tel: (071) 836 1973 and Centre for African Language Learning. Tel: (071) 240 0199. 38 King Street, London WC2E 8JT. Information on African language courses; courses in a number of African languages, notably Amharic, Shona and Swahili.

Albion House Language Centre, 23 Albion Street, Marble Arch, London W2 2AS. Tel: (071) 224 9771. Fax: (071) 224 9887.

All Languages Ltd, 362 Old Street, London EC1V 9LT. Tel: (071) 739 6641. Language training.

Alliance Française, 1 Dorset Square, London NW1 6PU. Tel: (071) 723 0020. French language courses.

Anglo-Austrian Society, 46 Queen Anne's Gate, London SW1H 9AU. Tel: (071) 222 0366. German language courses.

Association for Language Learning, 16 Regent Place, Rugby CV21 2PN. Tel: (0788) 546443. Association of language teachers.

Association of Language Export Centres, PO Box 1574, London NW1 4NJ. Tel: (071)) 224 3748.

Association of London Authorities, 36 Old Queen Street, London SW1H 9JF. Tel: (071) 222 7799. Publishes *Floodlight*, the official guide to part-time and evening classes in London.

Austrian Institute, 28 Rutland Gate, London SW7 1PW. Tel: (071)584 8653. Language courses in Austria.

Belstead House, Belstead, Ipswich. Tel: (0473) 686321. Short residential language courses.

Berlitz Language Centres, 79 Wells Street, London W1A 3BZ. Tel: (071) 580 6482. Language courses at schools throughout Britain and around the world.

Books in German, 6 Barnfield, Blackstone Edge Old Road, Littleborough, Lancs OL15 0JL. Tel: (0706) 72252. Mail-order service for German language books.

Appendix C

Brasshouse Centre, 50 Sheepcote Street, Birmingham B16 8AJ. Tel: (021) 643 0114. Language Export Centre.

Bristol Polytechnic, Coldharbour Lane, Frenchay, Bristol BS16 1QY. Tel: (0272) 656261. Language training.

Brintex Ltd, 32 Vauxhall Bridge Road, London SW1V 2SS. Tel: (071) 973 5054. Organisers of the London Language Fair.

British Association for Japanese Studies, Contemporary Japan Centre, University of Essex, Colchester CO4 3SQ. Tel: (0206) 872641. Summer intensive Japanese courses.

British–Bulgarian Friendship Society, c/o Finsbury Library, 245 St John Street, London EC1V 4NB. Tel: (071) 837 2304 — I. Purton. Information on Bulgarian courses.

British Council Specialist Tours Department, 10 Spring Gardens, London SW1A 2BN. Tel: (071) 930 8466. Summer language courses in Eastern Europe.

British–Romanian Friendship Association, 40 Brightwell Avenue, Westcliff-on-Sea, Essex SS0 9EE. Tel: (0702) 348161. Information on Romanian courses and language tutors.

Brunner Interlingua, 99–101 Worship Street, London EC2A 2BE. Tel: (071) 375 0040. Executive language training.

Burton Manor College, Burton, South Wirral, Cheshire L64 5SJ. Tel: (051) 336 5172. Language courses.

Business and Technician Education Council, Central House, Upper Woburn Place, London WC1H 0HH. Tel: (071) 388 3288.

Business Language Information Services (BLISS), 76 Colesbourne Drive, Downhead Park, Milton Keynes MK15 9AP. Tel: (0908) 607739. Consultancy and support service, especially for the multimedia Pitman/BBC courses '*Making your Mark*' and '*Franc Exchange*'.

Business Language Training, 42 Colebrook Row, London N1 8AF. Tel: (071) 226 2916. Company language training.

Cambridge Advisory Service, Rectory Lane, Kinston, Cambridge CB3 7NL. Tel: (0223) 264089. Language courses abroad.

Central Bureau for Educational Visits and Exchanges, Seymour Mews House, Seymour Mews, London W1H 9PE. Tel: (071) 486 5101; 3 Bruntsfield Crescent, Edinburgh EH10 4HD. Tel: (031) 447 8024; 16 Malone Road, Belfast BT9 5BN. Tel: (0232) 664418. Provides information and advice on all forms of educational visits and exchanges. Publishes *Home from Home*, *Study Holidays*, *Working Holidays* and a number of useful information sheets.

Centre for Information on Language Teaching and Research (CILT), Regent's College, Inner Circle, Regent's Park, London NW1 4NS. Tel: (071) 486 8221. Primarily a facility for language teachers, which can provide information on language courses to the general public. Publishes leaflets on specific languages. Some reference libraries may have copies of the now discontinued CILT *Language and Culture Guides*.

Centre for International Briefing, The Castle, Farnham, Surrey GU9 0AG. Tel: (0252) 721194. Short intensive language courses.

Cicero Languages International, 42 Upper Grosvenor Road, Tunbridge Wells TN1 2ET. Tel: (0892) 547077. Language training.

City and Guilds of London Institute, 46 Britannia Street, London WC1X 9RG. Tel: (071) 278 2468. An examining body for two modern language schemes: one primarily for use in schools; the other with a strong vocational bias. Languages: French, German, Italian, Spanish.

City Literary Institute, Stukely Street, Drury Lane, London WC2B 5LJ. Tel: (071) 242 9872. Adult education college with a wide range of language courses.

Coleg Harlech, Harlech, Gwynedd LL46 2PU. Tel: (0766) 780363. Residential courses in Welsh.

Comann Luchd Ionnsachaidh, 109 Church Street, Inverness. Tel: (0463) 234138. Information on Gaelic courses.

Communication and Executive Exchanges, 7 St Leonards Road, Exeter EX2 4LA. Tel: (0392) 75522. Intensive French courses.

Conrad Executive Language Training, 16 Henrietta Street, London WC2E 6QH. Tel: (071) 240 0855. Language training.

Council for African Languages and Culture, Southwark Council for Community Relations, 125 Camberwell Road, London SE5. Tel: (071) 252 7033. Information on courses and tutors.

Coventry Language Export Centre, Coventry Technical College, Butts, Coventry CV11 3GD. Tel: (0203) 256793.

Coventry Polytechnic, Priory Street, Coventry CV1 5FB. Tel: (0203) 631313. Language training.

Cultural and Educational Services Abroad (CESA), 44 Sydney Street, Brighton. Tel: (0273) 683304. Language courses abroad.

Danish Cultural Institute, 3 Doune Terrace, Edinburgh EH3 6DY. Danish courses.

Dante Aligheri Society, 61 Pond Street, London SW1X 0BG. Tel: (071) 823 8955. Italian courses.

Dilkington College, Ilminster, Somerset TA19 9DT. Tel: (0460) 52427. Residential language courses.

Dorset Business School, Holland House, Oxford Road, Bournemouth BH3 8EZ. Tel: (0202) 595400. Language training.

Dragons International, The Old Vicarage, South Newington, Banbury, Oxon OX15 4JN. Tel: (0295) 721991. Exchange holidays abroad.

Dundee University Centre for Continuing Education, Dundee DD1 4HN. Tel: (0382) 23181. Language training.

Ealing College of Higher Education: See Thames Valley University.

East Anglian Language Export Centre, 2 Looms Lane, Bury St Edmunds, Suffolk IP33 1HE. Tel: (0284) 764977.

East Midlands Language Export Centre (EMLEX), Charles Keen College, Painter Street, Leicester LE1 3WA. Tel: (0533) 516037.

Eaton Hall International, Retford, Notts. DN22 0PR. Tel: (0777) 706441. Language courses.

Ecosse Ltd (Language Export Centre), 5 Lynedoch Place, Glasgow G3 6AB. Tel: (041) 332 9886.

Appendix C

Edit 515 Ltd, 24 Buckstone Grove, Edinburgh EH10 6PF. Tel: (031) 445 1405. Language training through business games.
EF International Language Schools, 12 Junction Mews, Sussex Gardens, London W2 1PN. Tel: (071) 262 5708. Fax: (071) 402 5677. Language courses in UK (London, Brighton), Germany, France and Spain.
ELT Banbury, 49 Oxford Road, Banbury, Oxon OX16 9AH. Tel: (0295) 269522. Language courses abroad.
Esperanto Centre of Great Britain, 140 Holland Park Avenue, London W11 4UF. Tel: (071) 727 7821. Esperanto courses.
Euro-Academy Outbound, 77A George Street, Croydon CR0 1LD. Tel: (081) 681 2905. Courses abroad in various European languages.
Euro-Com, The Cornerstone, 42 Church Road, Smithills, Bolton BL1 6HE. Tel: (0204) 849849. Language training.
Euro-Japanese Exchange Foundation, EJEF Study Centre, Lane End, High Wycombe HP14 3HH. Tel: (0494) 882091. Japanese courses (part-time and intensive).
Eurolang Media Courses, 88 Wychwood Avenue, Knowle, Solihull, West Midlands B93 9DQ. Tel: (0564) 774452. In-company language training.
Europeople, 45B Blythe Street, London E2 6LN. Tel: (071) 729 5784. Language Club.
Executive Language Centre, Suite 311, Radnor House, Regent Street, London W1R 7TA. Tel: (071) 494 3851. Language training.
Exlingua International, 25 High Street, Belfast BT1 2AA. Tel: (0232) 235255. Language courses.
Finnish Bookshop, 28 Bute Street, London SW7 3EX. Tel: (071) 584 2840.
Foreign Language Services, 11 Lysander Grove, London N19 3QY. Tel: (071) 263 3996. Language courses.
French Institute (Institut Français), 14 Cromwell Place, London SW7 2JR. Tel: (071) 581 2701; 13 Randolph Crescent, Edinburgh EH3 7TT. Tel: (031) 225 5366. French courses.
The French Centre, Chepstow Lodge, 61–69 Chepstow Place, London W2 4TR. Tel: (071) 221 8134. French courses.
Glasgow University (Update Office), Glasgow G12 8QQ. Tel: (041) 330 5005. Language training.
Glenrothes College, Centre for Industrial Studies, Station Road, Fife KY6 2RA. Tel: (0592) 772233. Language Export Centre.
Globe Town Community Education Centre, Hadleigh Street, London E2 0LB. Tel: (081) 980 2588. In-company training and language centre.
Goethe Institut, 50 Princes Gate, London SW7 2PH. Tel: (071) 581 3344; 3 Park Circus, Glasgow G3 6AX. Tel: (041) 332 2555; Ridgefield House, 14 John Dalton Street, Manchester M2 6HG. Tel: (061) 834 4635; 86 Micklegate, York YO1 1JZ. Tel: (0904) 55222. Wide range of German courses.
Grafham Water Centre, Perry, Huntingdon PE18 0BX. Tel: (0480) 810521. Short residential language courses.

Grant and Cutler, 55–57 Great Marlborough Street, London W1V 2AY. Tel: (071) 734 2012. Bookshop specialising in European language books.

Grantley Hall, Ripon, North Yorkshire. Tel: (076) 586 259. Short residential language courses.

Greek Institute, 34 Bush Hill Road, London N21 2DS. Tel: (081) 360 7968.

Higham Hall, Bassenthwaite Lake, Cockermouth, Cumbria CA13 9SH. Tel: (059) 681 276. Short residential language courses.

Hispanic and Luso Brazilian Council, Canning House, 2 Belgrave Square, London SW1X 8PJ. Tel: (071) 235 2303. Portuguese courses.

Home Language International, 3 High Street, St Lawrence, Ramsgate CT11 0QL. Tel: (0843) 851116. Lessons abroad in teachers' homes.

Home Language Lessons, 2 Cecil Square, Margate CT9 1ED. Tel: (0843) 227700. Lessons abroad in teachers' homes.

Hull University (LIFT), Cottingham Road, Hull HU6 7RX. Tel: (0482) 466317. Language training.

Hungarian Language Services, 16 Kingswood Road, London W4 5ET. Tel: (081) 994 0517. Hungarian courses.

Inlingua, 28 Rotten Park Road, Birmingham. Tel: (021) 455 6465. Affiliated schools in Cheltenham and throughout the world.

Institute of Indian Culture, 4A Castletown Road, London W14 9GQ. Tel: (071) 381 3086. Information on courses in Indian languages.

Institute of Jewish Education, 44A Albert Road, London NW4 2SJ. Tel: (081) 203 6799. Hebrew courses.

Institute of Linguists, 24A Highbury Grove, London N5 2EA. Tel: (071) 359 7445. Examinations in foreign languages at five levels: Preliminary Certificate, General Certificate (equivalent to GCSE), Advanced Certificate (equivalent to 'A' Level), Intermediate Diploma and Diploma (equivalent to BA). Register of language teachers.

Intensive Language Training Specialists (ILTS), 44 City Business Centre, Lower Road, London SE16 2XB. Tel: (071) 231 5165. In-company language training.

Interlingua, Rothschild House, Whitgift Centre, Croydon CR9 3QT. Tel: (081) 688 3852. Executive language training.

International Business and Export Services, PO Box 64, Winchester SO23 8BG. Tel: (0962) 842533. Language Export Centre.

International Languages and Translations School, 1A Wilson Street, London N21 1BP. Tel: (081) 882 3362. Home language tuition.

International Links, 145 Manygate Lane, Shepperton, Middlesex TW17 9EP. Tel: (0932) 229300. Individual home stays in France, Germany, Italy, Russia and Spain.

International Punjabi Society, 202A Kensington High Street, London W8 5SE. Tel: (071) 937 4224. Information on Punjabi courses and tutors.

Interests Unlimited, 11 Winterbourne Avenue, Orpington, Kent BR6 9RH. Tel: (0689) 856162. Language Export Centre.

Appendix C

Intuition Languages, 109 Shepperton Road, London N1 3DF. Tel: (071) 359 7794. Language training.

Italian Bookshop (Accademia Italiana), 24 Rutland Gate, London SW7 1BB. Tel: (071) 225 3724.

Italian Institute, 39 Belgrave Square, London SW1. Tel: (071) 235 1461. Information on Italian language tuition.

Japan Business Consultancy, Newton Park, Bath BA1 9BN. Tel: (0225) 874146. Japanese courses.

Japan Centre, 5 Sherwood Street, London W1V 7RA. Tel: (071) 734 4422. Japanese language books and language tutors.

Japanese Language Association, Bath College of Higher Education, Newton Park, Bath BA2 9BN. Tel: (0225) 872170. Japanese tutor database.

Kendal College (TEAM), Milnthorpe Road, Kendal, Cumbria LA9 5AY. Tel: (0539) 724313. Language courses.

King's College Language and Communications Centre, Strand, London WC2R 2LS. Tel: (071) 873 2890. Language courses.

Kingston Language Export Centre, School of Languages, Kingston University, Penrhyn Road, Kingston-on-Thames KT1 2EE. Tel: (081) 547 2623.

Lancashire and Cumbria Language Export Centre, University of Central Lancashire, Preston, Lancs PR1 2TQ. Tel: (0772) 262232.

Lancashire College, Southport Road, Chorley, Lancs PR7 1NB. Tel: (0257) 276719. Language courses.

Language Centre of Guildford, 53 Woodbridge Road, Guildford GU1 4RF. Tel: (0483) 35118. Language training.

The Language Centre, Scotland, 7 Lauriston Gardens, Edinburgh EH3 9HH. Tel: (031) 229 9679. Language training.

The Language Learning Centre, 7 Kings Road, Reading RG1 3AR. Tel: (0734) 582247. Language courses.

LCL, 104 Judd Street, London WC1H 9NF. Tel: (071) 837 0487. Language bookshop with wide range of courses. Advice on course books.

Language Solutions Ltd, 16 Webbs Road, London SW11 1XJ. Tel: (071) 924 2166. Language training advice and placement.

Language Studies International, Woodstock House, 10–12 James Street, London W1M 5HN. Tel: (071) 499 9621. Language training. Centres also in Brighton and abroad.

Le Club Français Ltd, 18–19 High Street, Twyford, Winchester, Hants SO21 1RF. Tel: (0962) 7144036. Informal French teaching for children. Centres throughout Britain.

Leeds University Department for Continued Professional Education, Leeds LS2 9JT. Tel: (0532) 333241. Language training.

Richard Lewis Communications, Robins, Wood Lane, Bramdean, Alresford, Hants SO24 0JW. Tel: (0962) 771919. Language training in UK and abroad.

Linguarama, Queen's House, 8 Queen Street, London EC4. Tel: (071) 236 7206. Courses in a wide range of languages in UK and abroad.

Branches in Alton (Hants), Bath, Birmingham, Manchester, Stratford-on-Avon, Winchester and a residential centre at Ditteridge near Bath. Also 50 schools in Europe and Japan.

Linguaphone Institute, St Giles House, 50 Poland Street, London W1V 4AX. Tel: (071) 734 0574. Language training, including telephone tutorials.

Link Language Training, Albion House, 23 Albion Street, London W2 2AS. Tel: (071) 224 9771. Fax: (071) 706 8478. Executive language training.

London Language-Export Centre, Raine Tivers, 50–52 Putney Hill, London SW15 6QX. Tel: (081)780 0543.

London Centre for Pakistan Studies, ICIS House, 144–146 Kings Cross Road, London WC1X 9DH. Tel: (071) 833 8275. Urdu courses.

London Chamber of Commerce and Industry, Marlowe House, Station Road, Sidcup, Kent DA15 7BJ. Tel: (081) 302 0261. Organises secretarial examinations in French, German and Spanish as well as job-oriented oral examinations in the following foreign languages: Arabic, Bengali, Catalan, Chinese (Mandarin and Cantonese), Czech, Danish, Dutch, French, German, Gujarati, Hindi, Italian, Japanese, Norwegian, Polish, Punjabi, Russian, Serbo-Croat, Swedish, Urdu, Vietnamese, Welsh.

London Language Export Centre, 50–52 Putney Hill, London SW15 6QX. Tel: (081) 780 0543.

Lydbury Language-Export Centre, The Old Vicarage, Lydbury North, Salop SY7 8AU. Tel: (0588) 8233.

Managed Learning, Aston Science Park, Love Lane, Birmingham B7 4BJ. Tel: (021) 359 0981; Westminster College, Harcourt Hill, North Hinksey, Oxford OX2 9AS. Tel: (0865) 798188; 14 Queen's Square, Bath. Tel: (0225) 447163. Language Export Centre.

Manchester Business School Language Centre, Booth Street West, Manchester M15 6PB. Tel: (061) 275 6560. Language training.

Manchester Language Export Centre, Tatton Buildings, 6 Old Hall Road, Gatley, Cheadle, Cheshire SK8 4BE. Tel: (061) 428 3000.

Merseyside Language Export Centre, Modern Languages Building, University of Liverpool, Liverpool L69 3BX. Tel: (051) 794 2795.

Milton Keynes Language Centre, Chantry House, Watling Street, Fenny Stratford, Milton Keynes MK2 2BU. Tel: (0908) 225870. Language Export Centre.

Mind Management, 23 Sycamore Avenue, Hatfield, Herts AL10 8LZ. Tel: (0707) 264163. Accelerated language courses.

Missenden Abbey, Great Missenden, Bucks HP16 0BD. Tel: (0240) 66811. Short residential language courses.

Morley College Language Centre, 61 Westminster Bridge Road, London SE1 7HT. Language courses.

National Council for Educational Technology, Sir William Lyons Road, University of Warwick Science Park, Coventry CV4 7EZ. Tel: (0203) 416994. Organisation which promotes the use of IT in teaching. Produces useful information leaflets on language teaching software and IT vocabulary lists for French, German and Italian.

National Council for Mother Tongue Teaching, 52 Park Road, Rugby, Warwickshire CV21 2QH. Tel: (0788) 544516. Association which encourages the provision of community language teaching for children of ethnic minorities.

National Institute of Adult Continuing Education, 19B De Montfort Street, Leicester LE1 7GE. Tel: (0533) 551451. Publishers of *The Year Book of Adult Education*.

North-East Export Associates, University of Northumbria, Ellison Building, Ellison Place, Newcastle upon Tyne NE1 8ST. Tel: (091) 261 0190. Language Export Centre.

North-East Surrey College of Technology (Short Courses), Longmead Road, Epsom, Surrey KT17 3DS. Tel: (081) 394 1731. Language training.

Nottingham International Study Centre, Equitable House, South Parade, Old Market Square, Nottingham NG1 2LB. Tel: (0602) 473715. Language training.

North London University Language Services, Prince of Wales Road, London NW5 3LB. Tel: (071) 607 2789. Language training.

OMTRAC, The Clock House, North Street, Midhurst, West Sussex GU29 9DS. Tel: (0730) 815726. Operates a language training advisory and referral service established by the London Chamber of Commerce and Industry.

People First, 57 Highlands Road, Horsham, West Sussex RH13 5NE. Tel: (0403) 56790. In-company language training.

Polish Cultural Institute, 34 Portland Place, London W1H 4HQ. Tel: (071) 636 6032. Information on Polish courses in the UK and abroad.

Polyglot Language Services, Bennet Court, 1 Bellview Road, London SW17 2EG. Tel: (081) 767 9113. Language training.

Arthur Probsthain, 41 Great Russell Street, London WC1B 3PH. Tel: (071) 636 1096. Bookseller specialising in Oriental languages. Branch at School of Oriental and African Studies.

Professional Industrial and Commercial Updating (PICKUP), Room 2/2, Department of Education and Science, Sanctuary Building, Great Smith Street, London SW1P 3BT. Tel: (071) 925 5000. Co-sponsors (with Training Agency) of Language Export Centres.

Professional Language Studies, 53 Queens Gardens, Hyde Park, London W2 3AE. Tel: (071) 402 8605. Company language training.

Rapide Language Centres, 133 Chesterfield Road, St Andrews, Bristol BS6 5DU. Tel: (0272) 444114. In-company language training.

Reading College of Technology, Crescent Road, Reading RG1 5QQ. Tel: (0734) 583501. Language training.

Rendez-Vous, 25 Storey's Way, Cambridge CB3 0DP. Tel: (0223) 353595. In-company language training.

Ripon Language Services, University College of Ripon and York St John, College Road, Ripon, North Yorkshire HG4 2QX. Tel: (0765) 602691. Residential language training.

Robertson Languages International, 7 Grove Park, White Waltham, Maidenhead, Berks SL6 3LW. Tel: (0628) 829090. Language Export Centre.

RSA Examinations Board, Progress House, Westwood Way, Coventry CV4 8HS. Tel: (0203) 470033. Examinations in French, German, Italian and Spanish, including a new Certificate in Business Language Competence.

Safe Languages Ltd, 54A Brighton Road, Surbiton, Surrey KT6 5PL. Tel: (081) 399 9804.

Saint George International, 37 Manchester Street, London W1M 5PE. Tel: (071) 486 5481. Company language training.

Sandwell College of Further and Higher Education (Language Links), Woden Road South, Wednesbury, West Midlands WS10 0PE. Tel: (021) 556 6069. Language courses for industry.

School of Oriental and African Studies (SOAS), Thornhaugh Street, Russell Square, London WC1H 0XG. Tel: (071) 637 2388 (ext. 2536). Courses in all major African, Asian and Middle Eastern languages.

School of Slavonic and East European Studies (SSEES), University of London, Senate House, Malet Street, London WC1. Information on Slavonic and Baltic languages, Finnish and Hungarian.

SEE Europe Ltd, 1 Church Walk Studios, Beales Lane, Weybridge, Surrey KT13 8JS. Tel: (0932) 840440. Homestay language courses in Europe.

Services for Export and Language, Crescent House, University of Salford, Salford M5 4WT. Tel: (061) 745 7480. Language Export Centre.

SIBS Ltd, West Wing, Fen Drayton House, 5 Park Lane, Fen Drayton, Cambridgeshire CB4 5SW. Tel: (0954) 31956. Language courses abroad, especially Egypt, France, Germany, Italy, Portugual and Spain.

Society for Anglo-Chinese Understanding (Language Courses), 376 Rydal Road, London SW16 1QF. Tel: (081) 677 6110. Information on Chinese courses.

Society for Cultural Relations with the CIS, 320 Brixton Road, London SW9 6AB. Tel: (071) 274 2282. Organises a Russian course every Easter.

South Bank University Language Centre, Borough Road, London SE1 0AA. Tel: (071) 261 2529. Language training.

South Chesire College, External Relations Division, Dane Bank Avenue, Crewe, Cheshire CW2 8AB. Tel: (0270) 67923.

Spanish Institute, 102 Eaton Square, London SW1. Tel: (071) 235 1484. Spanish courses.

Speak-Easy Tele-language Ltd, HMS *President*, Victoria Embankment, London EC4Y 0HJ. Tel: (071) 936 2529. Language tuition by telephone.

Appendix C

Staffordshire Language-Export Centre, Business School, University of Staffordshire, College Road, Stoke on Trent ST4 2DE. Tel: (0782) 412143.

Stevenson College, Bankhead Avenue, Sight Hill, Edinburgh EH11 4DE. Tel: (031) 453 6161. Language training.

Surrey Language Centres, Sandford House, 39 West Street, Farnham, Surrey GU9 7BT. Tel: (0252) 733519. Language training.

Sussex and Kent Language Export Centre, The Language Centre, Brighton Polytechnic, Falmer, Brighton BN1 9PH. Tel: (0273) 679481.

Trade Management Institute, Temple Hill, Blackrock, Co. Dublin. Tel: Dublin 802984. Language training.

Thames Valley University, Languages for Business Unit, Grove House, 1 The Grove, London W5 5DX. Tel: (081) 579 5000. Language courses. Centre for Computer Assisted Learning.

Trinity Language Services, Glen House, 200–208 Tottenham Court Road, London W1P 9LA. Company language training.

Turkish Embassy (Education Department), Camelot House, 75 Brompton Road, London SW3 1EU. Tel: (071) 584 4062. Information on Turkish language courses.

Turkish Language Books, 81 Shacklewell Lane, London E8 2EB. Tel: (071) 249 0367. Turkish bookshop.

Universal Languages, 45 High Street, Kensington, London W8 5EB. Tel: (071) 938 1225. Language training.

University College London Language Centre, 134–136 Gower Street, London WC1E 6BT. Tel: (071) 380 7722. Language training including self access courses.

University of London School Examinations Board, Stewart House, 32 Russell Square, London WC1B 5DN. Tel: (071) 636 8000. Sets examinations in a wide range of languages. Past examination papers can be obtained from the University of London Publications Office, 52 Gordon Square, London WC1H 0PJ. Tel: (071) 636 8000.

University of the Third Age, 1 Stockwell Green, London SW9 9JF. Tel: (071) 737 2541. Informal courses in all subjects for retired people.

University of the West of England, Coldharbour Lane, Frenchay, Bristol BS16 1QY; Tel: (0272) 656261. Language training.

University of Westminster Language Centre, 9–18 Euston Centre, London NW1 3ET; Tel: (071) 911 5000. Language training including open access courses.

Valetti Corporate Language Training, 72 Queen Street, Maidenhead, Berks SL6 1HY. Tel: (0628) 23303. Language Training.

Wales Language and Export Training Centre, Science Tower, University College Swansea, Singleton Park, Swansea SA2 8PP. Tel: (0792) 295621.

Wales Language and Export Training Centre (North), Newtech Innovation Centre, Croesnewydd Hall, Wrexham Technology Park, Wrexham, Clwyd LL13 7YP. Tel: (0978) 295324.

Welsh Joint Education Committee (Welsh for Adults Officer), Welsh Department, 245 Western Avenue, Cardiff CF5 2YX. Database of Welsh tutors.

Welsh Language Society, Penroc, Rhodfair Mor, Aberystwyth. Tel: (0970) 624501. Information on Welsh courses.

Welsh Learners' Council, Adran y Gymraeg, University College of Wales, Old College, Aberystwyth SY23 2AX. Tel: (0970) 623111 (ext. 4052). Information on Welsh courses.

Western Language Centre, Forge House, Kemble, Glos GL7 6AD. Tel: (0285) 770447. Language training. Information on Suggestopedia.

Westminster Adult Education Institute, North Westminster School, Penfold Street, Paddington, London NW1. Tel: (071) 722 5151. Language courses.

Whiteley's International Language Centre, Whiteley House, 84 Miller Street, Glasgow G1. Tel: (041) 204 4152.

Windsor Languages, 21 Osborne House, Windsor, Berks SL4 3EG. Tel: (0753) 858995. Executive language training.

Wolverhampton Language Export Centre, Wolverhampton University, Stafford Street, Wolverhampton WV1 1SB. Tel: (0902) 322739.

Workers' Educational Association (WEU), Temple House, 9 Upper Berkeley Street, London W1H 8BY. Tel: (071) 402 5608.

Working Languages, 70 Mortlake Road, Kew Gardens, Richmond, Surrey TW9 4AS. Tel: (081) 675 9353. In-company language training.

World Language Consultants, Panton House, Panton Street, London SW1Y 4EN. Tel: (071) 930 3842. Language training.

Worth Consulting, 10 Nicholson Road, Loughborough, Leicestershire LE11 3SD. Tel: (0509) 263285.

Yorkshire and Humberside Export Services, Modern Languages Centre, Leeds Metropolitan University, Lawns Lane, Farnley, Leeds LS12 5ET. Tel: (0532) 630505. Language Export Centre.

Zionist Federation Educational Trust, Balfour House, 741 High Road, North Finchley N12 0BQ. Tel: (081) 446 1477; 142 Bury Old Road, Manchester M8 6HD. Tel: (061) 740 2864; 43 Queen Street, Glasgow. Tel: (041) 423 7379. Hebrew courses.

Appendix D
National Languages: A Country-by-Country Guide

Afghanistan: Pashto (Pushtu), Farsi (Persian)
Albania: Albanian
Algeria: Arabic, French
Andorra: Catalan, French, Spanish
Angola: Portuguese, Kimbundu, Umbundu, Chokwe, Kikongo
Argentina: Spanish, Quechua, Guarani
Armenia: Armenian
Austria: German
Azerbaijan:Azerbaijani
Bahamas: English
Bahrain: Arabic
Bangladesh: Bengali
Barbados: English
Belgium: French, Flemish (Dutch), German
Belize: English, Spanish
Benin: French, Fon, Fulani, Massi, Mine, Yoruba
Bermuda: English
Bhutan: Dzonga (Tibetan), Nepali
Bolivia: Spanish, Quechua, Aymara
Bosnia: Serbo-Croat
Botswana: English, Setswana (Sotho)
Brazil: Portuguese
Brunei: Malay, English, Chinese
Bulgaria: Bulgarian, Greek, Turkish
Burkina Faso: French, Bobo, Mossi, Gurma, Madingo, Fula, Senufo
Burma (Myanmar): Burmese, Shan
Burundi: Kirundi, French, Swahili
Cambodia: Khmer (Cambodian), French, Cham
Cameroon: French, English, Ewondo, Duala, Fanbula, Fula
Canada: English, French
Cape Verde: Portuguese, Creole
Cayman Islands: English
Central African Republic: French, Sango, Banda, Gbaya, Longala, Zande
Chad: French, Arabic, Sara, Kanuri, Sango
Chile: Spanish

China: Chinese
Colombia: Spanish
Comores Islands (Indian Ocean): Arabic, French, Comoran, Swahili, Malagasy
Congo: French, Kongo, Lingala, Kitubu, Kikongo, Teke
Costa Rica: Spanish
Cuba: Spanish
Cyprus: Greek, Turkish
Czech Republic: Czech, Slovak
Denmark: Danish
Djibouti: French, Arabic, Somali
Dominica: English
Dominican Republic: Spanish
Ecuador: Spanish, Quechua
Egypt: Arabic
El Salvador: Spanish, Nahuatl
Equatorial Guinea: Spanish, Fang, Bubi, Yoruba
Estonia: Estonian, Russian
Ethiopia: Amharic, Arabic, Tigrinya, Tigre, English
Fiji: English, Fijian, Hindi, Chinese
Finland: Finnish, Swedish
France: French, Breton
Gabon: French, Fang, Bantu languages
Gambia: English, Mandingo, Fulani, Wolof
Georgia: Georgian, Russian
Germany: German
Ghana: English, Ga, Hausa, Fanti, Twi (Akan), Ewe, Mossi, Senufo
Greece: Greek
Grenada: English
Guadeloupe: French
Guam: English, Chamorro, Japanese
Guatemala: Spanish, Mayan dialects
Guiana: French, Creole
Guinea: French, Malinke, Sussu, Fula
Guienea-Bissau: Portuguese, Creole, Mande, Fula
Guyana: English
Haiti: French, Creole
Honduras: Spanish
Hong Kong: English, Cantonese
Hungary: Hungarian
Iceland: Icelandic
India: Hindi, English, Bengali, Gujarati, Kannada, Marathi, Oriya, Punjabi, Telugu, Tamil, etc.
Indonesia: Indonesian, English, Javanese, Sundanese, Balinese, Achinese, Batak, Iban, Madurese, Sasak
Iran: Farsi (Persian)
Iraq: Arabic, Kurdish

Irish Republic: English, Irish
Israel: Hebrew, Arabic, Yiddish, English
Italy: Italian
Ivory Coast: French, Diula, Baula, Madingo, Kru, Senufo
Jamaica: English
Japan: Japanese
Jordan: Arabic, English
Kazakhstan: Kazakh, Russian
Kenya: English, Swahili, Kikuyu, Kamba, Luhya, Luo
Kirghizia: Kirghiz, Russian
Kiribati (Pacific): English, Gilbertan
Korea: Korean
Kuwait: Arabic
Laos: Lao, French
Latvia: Latvian, Russian
Lebanon: Arabic, French, English
Lesotho: English, Sesotho (Sotho)
Liberia: English, Kisi, Kru
Libya: Arabic, Berber
Liechtenstein: German
Lithuania: Lithuanian
Luxembourg: Letzeburgisch, French, German
Macedonia: Macedonian
Madagascar: Malagasy, French
Malawi: English, Chichewa, Nyanja
Malaysia: Malay, English, Chinese, Tamil
Maldives: Divehi (Sinhalese dialect), Arabic, English
Mali: French, Arabic, Bambara, Fula, Senufo
Malta: Maltese, English, Italian
Martinique: French, Creole
Mauritania: French, Arabic, Fulani, Parakole
Mauritius: English, French, Creole
Mexico: Spanish
Moldova: Moldavian (Romanian), Russian, Ukrainian
Mongolia: Mongolian, Russian
Morocco: Arabic, French, Spanish, Berber
Mozambique: Portuguese, Swahili, Macoa-Lomne, Tsonga, Chichewa, Nyanja, Shona
Namibia: Afrikaans, English, Orambo, Herero
Nepal: Nepali, Tibetan
Netherlands: Dutch
Netherlands: Antilles: Dutch, Papamiento, English, Spanish
New Caledonia: French
New Zealand: English, Maori
Nicaragua: Spanish, Miskito, Suno, English
Niger: French, Hausa, Fulani, Djerma-Songha, Tamashek, Kanuri
Nigeria: English, Yoruba, Hausa, Fulani, Ibo, Kanuri, Nupe, Tiv

Norway: Norwegian
Oman: Arabic
Pakistan: Urdu, Punjabi, Sindhi, Pashto, Baluchi, English
Panama: Spanish
Papua New Guinea: English, Pidgin, Motu
Paraguay: Spanish, Guarani
Peru: Spanish, Quechua
Philippines: Pilipino, English, Ilokano, Bikol, Cebuano
Poland: Polish
Portugal: Portuguese
Qatar: Arabic
Réunion: French, Creole
Romania: Romanian
Russia: Russian
Rwanda: Rundi, French, Swahili, Watutsi
St Kitts Nevis: English
St Lucia: English
St Vincent: English
Samoa: Samoan, English
So Tomé: Portuguese, Creole
Saudi Arabia: Arabic
Senegal: French, Wolof, Madingo, Diola
Seychelles: English, French, Creole
Sierra Leone: English, Temne, Mende, Krio
Singapore: English, Chinese (Putonghua), Malay, Tamil
Slovak Republic: Czechoslovak
Slovenia: Slovenian
Solomon Islands: English, Pidgin
Somalia: Somali, Arabic, English, Italian, Swahili
South Africa: English, Afrikaans, Zulu, Xhosa, Sesotho, Ronga
Spain: Spanish, Catalan, Basque
Sri Lanka: Sinhalese, Tamil, English
Sudan: Arabic, Luo, Zande
Surinam: Dutch, Spanish
Swaziland: English, Siswati
Sweden: Swedish
Switzerland: German, French, Italian, Rhaeto-Romanic
Syria: Arabic
Tadjikistan: Tadjik, Russian
Taiwan: Mandarin Chinese, Hakka, Amoy
Tanzania: Swahili, English, Luo, Rundi, Sukuma, Yao
Thailand: Thai
Togo: French, Ewe, Twi, Hausa, Kabre, Mossi, Yoruba
Tonga: English, Tongan
Trinidad and Tobago: English
Tunisia: Arabic, French
Turkey: Turkish

Turkmenistan: Turkmen, Russian
Tuvalu: English, Tuvaluan
Uganda: English, Swahili, Luganda, Luhya, Luo, Rundi
United Arab Emirates: Arabic
Uruguay: Spanish
Uzbekistan: Uzbek, Russian
Vanuatu (New Hebrides): Bislama, English, French
Venezuela: Spanish
Vietnam: Vietnamese
Yemen: Arabic
Yugoslavia: Macedonian, Serbo-Croat, Albanian
Zaïre: French, Amashi, Bemba, Lingala, Kingwana, Kikongo, Linda, Tshiluba, Swahili
Zambia: English, Nyanja, Bemba, Chichewa, Lozi, Luvale, Tonga, Chokwe, Luba
Zimbabwe: English, Shona, Chichewa, Ndebele, Nyanja, Ronga

HOW TO LIVE & WORK IN SAUDI ARABIA
Margaret Nydell & Joy McGregor

The book covers essential practical topics such as entry requirements, transport, money matters, housing, schools and insurance, plus vital pointers to Saudi Arabian values, customs, business practices and etiquette, providing a complete resource whether you are planning a stay or three months or three years. 'All in all I found this to be a fascinating and comprehensive guide.' *Phoenix/Association of Graduate Careers Advisory Services*. 'Commendably well written, and achieves an unusually high level of accuracy of information. The authors have adopted a sensible approach to expatriate living in the Kingdom, and their judgments and advice are balanced and shrewd. . . This book covers a lot of ground well.' *Middle East Association Information Digest*.

£8.99, 144pp illus. 1 85703 007 9.

Please add postage & packing (UK £1.00 per copy. Europe £2.00 per copy. World £3.00 per copy airmail).
How To Books Ltd, Plymbridge House, Estover Road, Plymouth PL6 7PZ, United Kingdom. Tel: (0752) 695745. Fax: (0752) 695699. Telex: 45635.

Appendix E
Select Bibliography

Azzopardi, E.: *Teach Yourself a Modern Language Quickly* (Angus & Robertson, 1980).
Ballhorn, F.: *Alphabets of the World* (Kemble Press, Banbury, 1983).
Campbell, G. L.: *Compendium of the World's Languages* (Routledge, 1991)
Comrie B (ed.): *The World's Major Languages* (Routledge, 1987).
Coulmas, Florian: *Writing Systems of the World* (Blackwell, 1989).
Hagen, S (ed.): *Languages in British Business — An Analysis of Current Needs* (University of Northumbria/CILT, 1988).
Hantrais, L.: *The Undergraduate's Guide to Studying Languages* (CILT, 1989).
Harley, A. F.: *Linguistics for Language Learners* (Macmillan, 1982).
Jones, R.: *How to Get a Job Abroad* ('How To' Books, 1991).
King, A.: *Degrees of Fluency — A Sixth Former's Guide to Language Degree Courses* (CILT, 1990).
King, A. and Thomas, G.: *Languages and Careers Information Pack* (CILT, 1989).
Lyall, Archibald: *Guide to 25 Languages of Europe* (Sedgwick & Jackson, 1984).
Pearce, G.: *'Bonjour, Europe' — Languages and the British Manager* (British Institute of Management, 1991).
Pimsleur, P.: *How to Learn a Foreign Language* (Heinle & Heinle, Boston, 1980).
Rose, L.: *Accelerated Learning* (Accelerated Learning Systems).
Stevick, E. W.: *Success with Foreign Languages* (Prentice Hall International, 1989).
Stork, F. C.: *So You Want to Learn a Language* (Faber & Faber, 1976).
Tinsley, T.: *How to Study Abroad* (Northcote House, 1990).

Courses for Leisure, Trotman & Co., 12–14 Hill Rise, Richmond, Surrey TW10 6UA. Tel: (081) 940 5668.
Floodlight (Association of London Authorities).
Foreign Languages at Work (London Chamber of Commerce and Industry).
Guide to Language Courses in Polytechnics and Similar Institutions (Standing Conference of Heads of Modern Languages, University of Central Lancashire, Preston PR1 2TQ).
Home from Home (Central Bureau).

Language Travel Gazette, 10 Wright's Lane, London W8 6TA. Tel: (071) 930 3842.

Languages and your Career (Institute of Linguists)

Older Learners — The Challenge of Adult Education, Help the Aged, PO Box 460, St James's Walk, London WC1R 0BE. Tel: (071) 253 0253.

Study Abroad (UNESCO).

Study Holidays (Central Bureau).

Summer Academy: Study Holidays at British Universities, School of Continuing Education, University of Kent, Canterbury CT2 7NX. Tel: (0227) 470402.

Time to Learn, National Institute of Continuing Education, 19B De Montfort Street, Leicester LE1 7GE. Tel: (0533) 551451.

Where and How? — The Global Guide to Language Centres (Wie und Wo Verlag).

Working in Languages (COIC).

Working with Languages: which languages shall I learn? (Institute of Linguists).

Appendix F
Language Families

This section lists some of the major language groups. Clearly if you know a language belonging to the same group, you will master it more speedily.

INDO-EUROPEAN

Sub-group	
CELTIC	Irish, Gaelic, Welsh, Breton
GERMANIC (NORTH)	Swedish, Danish, Icelandic, Norwegian
GERMANIC (WEST)	English, Dutch, German, Afrikaans, Yiddish
ROMANCE	Latin, Italian, French, Spanish, Portuguese, Romanian
BALTIC	Latvian, Lithuanian
SLAVONIC (EAST)	Russian, Ukrainian, Belorussian (White Russian)
SLAVONIC (SOUTH)	Bulgarian, Slovenian, Serbo-Croat
SLAVONIC (WEST)	Czech, Slovak, Polish
ALBANIAN	Albanian
GREEK	Ancient Greek, Modern Greek
ARMENIAN	Armenian
IRANIAN	Persian, Pashto, Kurdish, Baluchi
INDO-ARYAN	Assamese, Hindi, Bengali, Gujarati, Marathi, Nepali (Pahari), Panjabi, Oriya, Singhalese, Urdu, etc.

URALIC

FINNO-UGRIC	Finnish, Estonian, Karelian
UGRIC	Hungarian

TURKIC

Turkish, Azerbaijani, Turkmen

AFRO-ASIATIC

EGYPTIAN	Coptic
SEMITIC	Arabic, Hebrew, Amharic, Tigre, Tigrinya
CUSHITIC	Somali
OMOTIC	Languages of Omo Valley, Ethiopia
BERBER	Berber
CHADIC	Hausa, Mandara, Masa

DRAVIDIAN

SOUTH	Tamil, Malayalam, Kannada, Kota
SOUTH CENTRAL	Telugu, Pengo, Manda, Gondi, Kui
CENTRAL	Kolami, Maiki
NORTH	Kurux, Malto, Brahui

SINO-TIBETAN

SINITIC	Chinese: Mandarin (Putonghua), Wu, Min, Yue (includes Cantonese), Hakka
TIBETO-BURMAN	Tibetan, Burmese, Karen

AUSTRONESIAN

WESTERN	Malay/Indonesian, Javanese, Achinese, Balinese, Tagalog (Pilipino), Malagasy
CENTRAL EASTERN	Samoan, Tongan, Fijian, Tahitian, Maori, Chamorro, Tolai, Motu

NIGER-CONGO

EAST ATLANTIC	Fula, Serer, Wolof, Dyola, Balante, Kissi, Gola, Limba
MANDE	Maninke, Bambara, Mende, Sininke, Kpelle, Samo, Busa
VOLTAIC (GUR)	Mossi (More), Dagari, Dagomba, Lobiri, Tem, Bariba
KWA	Akan (Twi), Ewe, Yoruba, Igbo, Grebo

BENUE-CONGO	Bantu (Swahili, Shona, Tswana, Sotho, Luganda, Zulu, Xhosa, Gikuyu, Rundi, etc.), Efik-Ibibio, Tiv
ADAMAWA-EASTERN	Gbaya, Banda, Zande

Index

Note that figures refer to page numbers and letters to the relevant appendix.

ability, 26, 49
abstractors, 15–16
academic language, 11
Advanced (A) Level, 28, 65, 73
adult education centres, 27, 29–30, 76
Africa, 10, 12, 20
Africa Centre, 31, C
Afrikaans, A
aims, 15, 26, 85
Albanian, A
alphabets, 19, 46–47, 66
Amharic, A
Angola, 22, D
aptitude, 49
Arab World, 12, 18
Arabic, 17, 18, 27, 47, A
Armenian, A
art, 21
Asia Minor, 23
Assamese, A
assessment, 27–28, 60–62, 65, 92–93, 108–109
Association of Graduate Careers Advisory Services (AGCAS), 56
Association of London Authorities, 29, C, E
audio cassettes, 50, 51, 62, 75, 77
au pair, 79
Australasia, 9, 14
Austria, 21, D

Bacon R, 10
Basque, A
Bengali, 17, 24, A
Berlitz M, 31, 42
bi-lingualism, 75, 80
booksellers, 34, 50, 81, C

Brazil, 22, D
Breton, A
Bristol University, 30
British Broadcasting Corporation (BBC), 16, 38, 50, 75, 77, B
British Institute of Management, 82
British Overseas Trade Board (BOTB), 65
Bulgarian, A
Burma (Myanmar), 24, D
Burmese, A
business, 9, 11, 82–83
Business and Technician Education Council (BTEC), 82, C
business language courses, 32, 50, 82–93
business links, 11, 82

Cambodian (Khmer), 47, A
Canada, 14, D
Canterbury Tales, 39
Cantonese, 18–19 (see Chinese)
career, 14–15
Careers and Occupational Information Centre (COIC), 56
careers with languages, 15–16, 56
Caribbean, 23
Catalan, A
Central Bureau for Educational Visits and Exchanges, 34, 64, 69, 71, 78, 79, C, E
Centre for Information on Language Teaching (CILT), 50, 56, 62, 71, C
Centre for International Briefing, 90, C
certificate of competence, 65
challenge, 13
Chamorro, A

155

Chaucer, G, 37
children, 73–81
China, 18–19, D
Chinese, 17, 118–19, 27–30, 41, 47, A
Chinese people, 18–19, 25, 37–38
City and Guilds of London Institute, 92, C
Club Français, 75, C
Coleg Harlech, 30, C
community colleges, 29–30
compact discs, 63, 77
company language training, 82–93
competence, 58, 87, 92
computer, 15
computer games, 78
constraints, 26, 28, 88
continuing education departments, 30–31
Cornish, 17, 29, A
correspondence colleges, 33
Corsican, A
cosmopolitanism, 15
cost, 50–52, 70
Council for the Accreditation of Correspondence Colleges (CACC), 33, C
course books, 36, 50, A, B
course fees, 50-52, 70
course providers, 28–35, 90, 91
Courses for Leisure, 30
Creole, A
cultural briefings, 90
cultural links, 11
cultural organisations, 31, 65, 81, C
culture, 11
customer, 11, 85, 86
Czechoslovak, 23, A

Danish, A
dialects, 68
dictionaries, 44–45, 76–77
Direct Method teaching, 52
distance learning, 33, 77
documentation, 12, 22
duration of course, 26–27
Dutch, A

East Asia, 19
Eastern Europe, 23
Educational Centres Association, 29
embarrassment, 53

employers, 14–15, 82–93
English, 9, 17, 24, 37–43, 82–83
enrolment, 29
enthusiasm, 72–73
ERASMUS, 71
Esperanto, 43, A
Estonian, A
ethnic minorities, 14, 24, 62, 81
ethnic minority languages, 14, 29
Euro-Academy, 34, 79, C
Europe, 10, 82
European Commission, 71, 79
examinations, 26, 28
examination boards, 65, 92, C
exchanges, 11, 23, 69, 74, 78–79
expatriates, 80–81
extra-mural study departments, 30–31

Farsi, see Persian, A
films, 77–78
Finnish, 17, A
Flemish, see Dutch, A
Floodlight, 29, A, E
foreign businessmen, 10
Foreign Languages at Work Scheme (FLAW), 65, 92
foreign texts, 11–12
foreign visits, 63, 68–70, 78–80
French, 10, 17, 20–23, 37, 39, 42, 44, 75, A
French Institute, 31, C
frequency of lessons, 26–27, 53–54
Fula, A
further education (FE) colleges, 28–29, 91

Gaelic, 24, A
gender, 43, 46
General Certificate of Secondary Education (GCSE), 26, 65, 73
generalisation, 47
German, 10–17, 20–21, 42, 43, 44, A
Germanic languages, 41, 44, 45, F
Germany, 20–21, D
gesture, 54
Glosa, A
Goa, 22
Goethe Institut, 31
Government Communications HQ (GCHQ), 16
grammar, 42–45

Grebo, A
Greek, 9, 14, 23, 47, A
Gujarati, A

Hagen S, 92
Hantrais, L, 30, 71
Hausa, 24, A
Hawaiian, A
Hebrew, A
Help the Aged, 62
higher education (HE) colleges, 30–31, 91
Hindi, 17, 24, A
holidays, 13, 68–69, 78–79
Home from Home, 69
Home Language Lessons, 34, C
Hungarian, 23, A

Ibo, A
Icelandic, A
Indonesian, 24, A
in-house courses, 53, 82–93
Inlingua, 32, C
insight, 13
Institute of Indian Culture, 31, C
Institute of Linguists, 28, 65, 92, C
intellect, 13
intelligence, 27, 49–50
intensive language courses, 14, 27, 28, 19, 31, 32, 55–56, 57, 70, 90
interactive videos, 55, 62–63
International Baccalaureate, 79
International Links, 78, C
international organisations, 11
International Phonetic Alphabet (IPA), 38, 40
international understanding, 12
interpreters, 11
interpreting, 15
intonation, 39–42
Irish Gaelic, 24, A
Irish Republic, 10, 24, D
Islam, 18
isolation, 13
Italian, 10, 21–22, 27, 54, 68, A

Japanese, 12, 17, 19–20, 46, A
Japanese people, 12, 19–20
Jobcentres, 29

Kannada, A

keeping up, 56–57
Khmer, see Cambodian, A
King's College, London, 30, C
Korean, 24, A
Kurdish, A

language clubs, 64, C
language consultants, 88–89
Language Export Centres, 90, C
Language International, 10
language laboratories, 42, 55
language of business, 10, 83
language schools, 31–32, 35, 70, 76
language skills, 26, 66, 85–86
language teachers, 26, 36–37, 42
language teaching in primary schools, 75
Language Travel Gazette, 34, E
language variations, 68
Languages Lead Body, 92
Lao, A
Latin, 14, 22, 23, 45, A
Latvian, A
learning environment, 36, 53
learning handicaps, 54–55
learning methods, 36
learning problems, 36
length of course, 26–27
Letzeburgesch, A
levels of competence, 57–59, 60–61, 87
libraries, 29, 32, 51, 63, 77, 81
LINGUA, 79
lingua franca, 10, 20, 21
Linguaphone, 33, B, C
linguistic hurdle, 13
listening, 44, 66
literature, 12, 20, 21, 22
Lithuanian, A
London Chamber of Commerce and Industry (LCCI), 58, 60–61, 65, 92, C
London University, 27, C
Luxembourgish see Letzeburgesch, A

Macao, 22
machine translation, 15
Malay, 24, A
Malayalam, A
Maltese, A
managers, 15, 82–83, 90

Manchester Business School, 27
Manx, 17
Maori, A
Marathi, A
Mende, A
mature learners, 59–60
measuring competence, 92
memory, 55
mental blocks, 64
methodology, 36, 37, 42, 50
Middle Ages, 22
mistakes, 53, 64
mixed ability classes, 74
mnemotechnics, 46
monitoring, 15
motivation, 27, 49, 55, 72
motives, 16
Mozambique, 22, D
music, 21

national attitudes, 12
national boundaries, 9
National Council for Mother Tongue Teaching, 81
National Curriculum (UK), 73
National Extension College, 33, B
National Institute of Continuing Education, 30, C
National Training Directory, 31
negotiation, 11
Nepali, A
newspapers, 12, 63–64, 66, 77
nouns, 43–44, 47
Norman French, 20, 45
North America, 9, 14
Norwegian, A

Omaggio, A, 66–67
official languages, 17, 20
one to one tuition, 67, 70, 89
open access learning, 29, 89
Open College, 33
Open University, 33, 59
oral competence, 26
Oriya, A

Pakistan, 25, D
parents, 73–81
Pashto see Persian, A
passive understanding, 11
pen friends, 77

Persian, 24, 47, A
persistence, 48, 64
phonemes, 37–39, 40, 46–47
phonetics, 37–39, 40
phrase books, 51, 76–77
Pidgin, A
Pilipino, A
Polish, 23, A
political links, 11
Portugal, 22, D
Portuguese, 10, 17, 22, A
practice, 63
prepositions, 43
primary schools, 75
private language schools, 31–32, 70, 76, 91, C
private tutors, 67–68, 76
Professional, Industrial and Commercial Updating (PICKUP), 91, C
professional organisations, 11
proficiency, 26–27
progress reports, 92
pronunciation, 37–42
public sector bodies, 11
publishers, 51, B
Punjabi, A

qualifications, 28, 65, 89, 92
Quechua, A

radio, 13, 50, 64, 77
reading skills, 26, 66
recreation, 13, 28
Renaissance, 21
research, 11–12
residence abroad, 12–13, 79, 80, 90
residential colleges, 30, 34
residential courses, 55–56, 82
Romance languages, 20, 44, 45, F
Romanian, A
Romany, 28
Royal Society for the Encouragement of the Arts, Manufactures and Commerce (RSA), 58–59, 65, 92, C
Russian, 17, 22–23, A

sales people, 11, 83
Samoan, A
Sanskrit, A

Index

School of Oriental and African Studies (SOAS), 31, 90, C
scientific publications, 11–12, 19–20
scholarships, 71
Scotland, 24, 75
selection for language training, 84–89
self-consciousness, 38
self study, 33–34, 55, 89
Serbo-Croat, 23, A
Shakespeare W, 10, 49
Shan, see Thai, A
Shona, A
Siamese, see Thai, A
SIBS, 34, 79, C
simplified texts, 66
Sinhalese, A
Slavonic, 22–23
Slovenian, A
Society for Anglo-Chinese Understanding (SACU), 31, C
Somali, A
Sotho, A
South America, 10, 23
South East Asia, 14
Spanish, 10, 17, 23, A
Spanish Institute, 31, C
Speak-Easy, 33, C
speech habits, 38, 66
standard language, 68
starting a course, 36–37
state schools, 27, 73–74, 75
Steadman H, 56
Stevick E, 50, 64
stress patterns, 41–42
Study Holidays at British Universities, 31, E
studying abroad, 34–35, 70, 78–79, 90
successful language learner, 76–77
survival languages, 52, 78–79
Swahili, 24, A
Swedish, A
Switzerland, 21, D

Tagalog see Pilipino, A
tailor-made courses, 89
Tamil, A
teachers, 26, 36, 37, 65, 67–68, 84
teaching as a career, 16
teaching environment, 36, 53
teaching techniques, 36–37, 42, 73–74
technical colleges, 28–29

technical staff, 11
technology for language learning, 62–63
telephone tutorials, 33, 89
television courses, 50, 77, see also BBC
Telugu, A
tenses, 48–49
Thai, 24, 41, 47, A
Threshold Level, 50, 60
Tibetan, A
Tigrinya, 29
tonal languages, 41
'top ten' languages, 17–23, 88
Training Access Points (TAP), 29, 91
Training Agency, 29, 91
training consultants, 88–89, C
training organisations, 90, 91–92, C
transcription, 47, 66
translating, 15, 47
travel, 13, 63, 68–70, 71, 78–79
Turkey, 9, D
Turkish, 23, 43–44, A
'Twelfth Night', 49
Twi, A
'twinning' arrangements, 11, 77, 78

Ukrainian, A
undergraduates, 30
understanding, 68
UNESCO, 34, 64
universities, 30–31
University College of Wales, 31, C
University of the Third Age, 32, 62, C
Urdu, 17, 24, 47, A
US Foreign Service Institute, 33–34, B

vacation, 13, 64
Vacation Work, 64, 71
van Deth J-P, 10
verbs, 44–45, 47
video cassettes, 50, 62–63, 75, 77–78
Vietnamese, 24, 41, A
visits abroad, 34–35, 63, 68–69, 78–80, 89–90
vocabulary, 45–46, 66

Wales, 49, 75
Waystage Level, 58
weekend courses, 30
Welsh, 75, A
Where and How?, 32, 34, 79, B, E

Workers' Educational Association, 31, C
working abroad, 69–70, 90
world radio, 64
writing skills, 26, 66
writing systems, 19, 46–47, 66

Xhosa, A

Yellow Pages, 32
Yiddish, A
Yoruba, A
young learners, 59, 70–71, 73–81

zeal, 71–72
Zulu, A